R

AM
LOST &
FOUND

BY THE SAME AUTHOR

FICTION
Making Progress
The Mother Tongue
Major André

NONFICTION
The Inside Passage
Through the Great City
The Thousand Dollar Yacht
The Light in Holland
In the Village
A Concise History of the Low Countries
Rembrandt's House
Acts of Union
Along the Edge of the Forest
Spring Jaunts
The Outer Banks
A Walk through Wales
The Coast of Summer
Responses to Rembrandt
Standing in the Sun: A Life of J. M. W. Turner

AUTOBIOGRAPHY
America, Lost & Found
England, First & Last

Anthony Bailey

AMERICA, LOST & FOUND

The University of Chicago Press

The University of Chicago Press, Chicago 60637
Copyright © 1980 by Anthony Bailey
Afterword © 2000 by Anthony Bailey
All rights reserved. Originally published 1981 by Random House, Inc.
University of Chicago Press edition 2000

Portions of this work have previously appeared
in *The New Yorker.*

*Grateful acknowledgment is made to the following
for permission to reprint material:*
The Condé Nast Publications, Inc.: Photograph of
Eloise and Otto Spaeth by Serge Balkin. Courtesy
Vogue, Copyright 1950 (renewed 1978), The Condé Nast
Publications, Inc.

Printed in the United States of America
05 04 03 02 01 00   6 5 4 3 2 1

Library of Congress Cataloging-in-Publication Data

Bailey, Anthony
America, lost & found / Anthony Bailey.
p. cm
ISBN 0-226-03455-0 (paper : alk. paper)
1. Bailey, Anthony—Childhood and youth.   2. World War,
1939–1945—Evacuation of civilians—England.   3. Bailey,
Anthony—Homes and haunts—Ohio—Dayton.   4. Authors,
English—20th century—Biography.   5. World War, 1939–1945—
Ohio—Dayton.   6. British—Ohio—Dayton—Biography.   7. World
War, 1939–1945—Children.   8. Dayton (Ohio)—Biography.
I. Title: America, lost & found.   II. Title.
PR6052.A3184 Z462 2000
977.1'73—dc21   99-057692

This book is printed on acid-free paper.

to those who sent us
and to those who
took us in

AMERICA,
LOST &
FOUND

|| 1 ||

SHAKING HANDS WAS AN ACTIVITY THAT SEEMED TO PUNC-tuate my life between the ages of seven and eleven. I attempted to shake hands with my father as he hugged me, in the course of saying goodbye behind sandbagged windows in Upper Grosvenor Street, London, before I joined a departing group of similarly blue-gabardine-raincoated, gas-mask-bearing, identity-tagged youngsters in the care of a young woman who was working for an American committee evacuating children from Europe. It was her hand I shook next and again a few weeks later, at the end of a voyage that had taken me by train to Liverpool, by an upright old Cunard White Star liner named *Antonia* in convoy to Montreal, and by train to New York. I shook hands with various celebrities who came, purportedly to cheer us up, to the home for found-lings in the Bronx where we were quartered while volun-teer families from all over the United States turned up to collect us and look after us—for a while, for the duration of the war, or maybe, if need be, forever. (The name of Douglas Fairbanks Jr., one of the visitors, had to be ex-plained to me. When it had been, I was disappointed by his failure to carry on in a swashbuckling manner; a firm hand-shake and an autograph were not enough.) I shook hands on the platform of the railroad station of Dayton, Ohio, before the Speed Graphic of the Dayton *Journal-Herald*'s photographer, with a small American boy who, I had been told, was almost exactly one year my junior, whose name like mine was Tony, but whose gray shorts were exotically shorter than the boxy type I wore, the bottoms of their legs just brushing my kneecaps. DAYTON WELCOME FOR YOUNG BRITISH WAR HEROES, said the *Journal-Herald* the next day over a column of cheerful twaddle, incorporating some of my and my companions' stiff-upper-lip responses to their reporter's questions about Hitler and bombs. Behind the American Tony's welcoming smile there might rightfully have lurked a wariness of the foreign intruder. And although I was soon fully fitted in as his foster brother, within the year wearing De Pinna shorts as short as his, treated by his parents in the way of presents, schools, food and spankings as another son, with my accent rapidly modified by mid-America, I was also at frequent intervals hauled out of that state of camouflage or transhumance to resume for a moment or so my aboriginal identity. "This is our little English boy." "This is our English Tony." "This is Tony Bailey from England, who is staying with us for the war."

I shook hands with family friends, distinguished visitors such as the Papal Nuncio, generals of the Army Air Corps, and foreign painters, and as I did so bowed slightly from the waist (in the way that Tony Spaeth and I were soon taught), and did my best to follow instructions by looking whomever I was introduced to in the eye—though at that age, it meant raising my eyes considerably from where they fell, on an adult, at about mid-chest level. I shook hands with James, the Spaeths' Negro butler-chauffeur, and immediately made him laugh by asking him if he was an American Indian. (I knew about the Wild West but not about slavery. Columbus had made a similar mistake, and by misidentifying the natives he found in the Western hemisphere, had laid the grounds for my confusion.) I shook hands with other children who were in the same boat as myself, my fellows in fortunate exile, as we were brought together at Christmas parties to record messages on steel discs for home or simply found ourselves on hand and there together when our hosts met for drinks or dinner. "Wilfrid, this is Tony Bailey, who's also from England." But then, since my foster parents were too sensible to imagine that that "also" would span a three-year difference in age, and perhaps knew themselves how origin and the state of being away from home, factors in common, might in many circumstances be positively divisive, there would follow a flurry of embarrassment-ridding demands: "Wilfrid, if you will go and see whether Miss Sjolin has got Mimi ready to come down . . ." "Tony Bailey, you pass the peanuts around to the grownups and then help Uncle Otto serve the drinks."

Marta Sjolin was the Swedish governess who quit ("I cannot stand the Dayton climate") or was fired by Mrs. Spaeth ("She insists on telling me how to raise my children") in Chatham, on Cape Cod, in August 1941, where we had all gone for the summer, only a few weeks after I had shaken hands with her brother—a merchant marine officer whose ship had called at Boston, and whose visit perhaps roused in Miss Sjolin longings that might be assuaged in part by a new post in Massachusetts. New England reminded her of Sweden. She embraced me, gripping me so that my hands could do no shaking, and so—though I would have done so anyway—I kissed her, saying goodbye. On several occasions I was made to shake hands after spontaneous fights with the other Tony. I shook hands, as all contestants did, on going into the ring at camp in Michigan for the "Midget" boxing finals, or at any rate mimicked the action, gloved paws bouncing off those of my determined-looking but possibly equally scared opponent while the Director of Sports muttered, "Okay, you guys, make it a good clean fight now!" Several times in my imagination, that first winter away from home, lying in bed recovering from what seemed to be a winter-long

attack of whooping cough, I shook hands with Mr. Churchill and Mr. Roosevelt as they recognized my contribution
to the war effort through my invention of armor-plated
barrage balloons or submarines that sprouted wings. At
the end of four years I shook hands on saying farewell to
innumerable people in Dayton—with teachers, fellow first-
year junior-high students, customers on my paper route,
the parish priest, James and Tony Spaeth, and then, a
fortnight later, with the officers of the aircraft carrier that
had brought a small group of us, evacuees to America, back
to Britain. Finally I put out my hand to shake that of the
woman, with premature streaks of gray hair, who met me
in Glasgow, who I thought might be my aunt, but who,
as she put her arms around me, I realized was my mother.

|| 2 ||

THE SPAETHS' HOUSE, AND MY HOME FOR THOSE FOUR YEARS, was 630 Runnymede Drive. The largesse of America seemed implicit in that address. No house I knew in England had a number that high, or suggested as this did a street that wound into the farthest reaches of the suburb of Oakwood, lined with homes of varied grandeur. (In fact the street numbers, often going up in bounds of 15 or 20, related to a city numbering system that enabled one to tell where a house on a minor road was in relation to one of the main Dayton streets, going north, east, south or west.) At that time I didn't know about the field by the Thames in England where the barons demanded and got a written agreement from King John on the rights of freeborn Englishmen. In Oakwood, however, I was at once aware of the liberty of being able to play on Talbott Hill, the undeveloped greensward across Runnymede Drive from 630. And the house itself made an immediate impression on me—I took to it faster than to its inhabitants, perhaps because it made no demands on my shyness but gave roof and room to all sorts of moods, both enthusiasms and reserve. It didn't need answers to questions or polite smiles; it was immensely, tacitly, accommodating. And even now, when experience has confirmed that many things that seemed large to one as a child are a good deal smaller, at least in adult scale, 630 Runnymede remains undiminished in my mind—a mansion.

Of course I compared it with what I knew, an average English house. The example closest to me then was the poky bungalow—situated in an unpaved Hampshire country lane—that I had just left, and which I could picture only in association with my mother standing with my three-year-old sister Bridget on the steps by the front gate, waving goodbye to me and my father as we set off for London. We had lived in Edenholme (the bungalow's name) for only a few months, but it was more spacious than the flat—upstairs over the bank my father managed—that had been our previous home. This was in Portchester, a small town at the head of Portsmouth harbor, distinguished by having one of the finest castles in Britain, on whose walls, moats and keeps the Romans, Saxons and Normans had worked. But Portchester, my father thought, was not far enough away from the modern naval installations and warships that made Portsmouth a prime target for air raids. Edenholme, in a hamlet called Park Gate, was about as distant into the country as you could get on the twenty-mile-long coastal stretch between Portsmouth (my birthplace) and the commercial seaport of Southampton (also a target), while still being near the railway which took him to work and could take me to school. Edenholme had rooms barely big enough to accommodate the furniture put in them; but apart from the merits of its location it had a long, high-hedged garden with an orchard of thirty fruit trees—apples named Worcester, Blenheim and Bramley—and an extensive lawn. Part of this had recently been sacrificed for a reinforced-concrete air-raid shelter, a luxury my father could hardly afford on his bank salary but which, taking the war seriously, he decided was safer than the two standard models on offer, free to most people: the Morrison shelter, a sturdy-looking steel table with wire-mesh sides to roll down once you'd crawled underneath, and named after Herbert Morrison, the Minister of Home Security (this was the kind my mother's parents had in their dining room in Southampton), and the Anderson shelter (Sir John Anderson was Home Secretary), a corrugated-steel outdoor model that, often with a covering layer of turf, was being erected in backyards and gardens all over the country.

One thing 630 Runnymede had in common with Edenholme—it was built of brick, a material I later realized was less than usual in America. Like the replicas of châteaux the industrial barons of the New World plumped down in Newport, Rhode Island, as cottages within invidious spitting distance of one another, rather than as stately homes in grand seclusion, 630 sat on a relatively small plot of land, un-fenced or -walled, on the slope of the hill that Runnymede Drive (also, unusually, brickpaved) at this point climbed. The house was separated from its equally large neighbors above and below by shrubs, trees and a concrete driveway. Among other, more expected rooms, it had a butler's pantry, a maid's room, a governess' room, a billiard room, and a laundry, served by a laundry chute. Of the novelties in the house, this intrigued me the most. Access to it was by way of a cupboard door on an upstairs landing. Open the door, and there was a galvanized-steel orifice, about eighteen inches square, the opening of a tunnel that sloped downward for ten feet and then fell vertically, past the kitchen, into the basement, where it emptied into a large hopper made of wooden slats. Dirty clothes and linen were stuffed into the chute and then disappeared, slowly at first, then accelerating with a pleasant hiss of cotton against metal, landing without sound in the laundry room below. It was almost as if one were getting rid of the clothes forever—a magical process (in which a black woman called Mabel, who came several days a week, had a part) that brought them back to shelves and drawers, clean, pressed and folded. The laundry chute was also a challenge. "I dare you to" was one of the first American phrases that registered with me, and which I took up. It was one of the benefits of having an as-it-were brother, and pretty soon Tony Spaeth and I were daring each other to do various things. ("I dare you to hide Miss Sjolin's slippers." "I dare you to stick your finger in that mess"—whatever it was—"and taste it".) We dared each other to go down the laundry chute. Sliding down might have been repugnant for a seven-year-old who had recently spent eight nights in a porthole-less ship's cabin belowdecks and, before that, been forced to sleep occasionally in a small air-raid shelter smelling closely of damp concrete. But no. We went down feet first, with a swish, and landed suddenly and softly on a pile of sheets in the hopper. The sport was quickly forbidden, once discovered. Fears of small but growing boys getting stuck and the house having to be pulled apart to get at them while they hung there . . .

But this is to plunge through 630, feet first. Starting again, by the front door, which was side-lit by tall, narrow windows, one walked into a wide hall. On the left a double-width doorway opened into the dining room; in front, against the left wall, a staircase, with wider steps at the bottom, curved upward (the wallpaper had a neo-classical motif of little ruined temples, sylvan glades, disporting nymphs and pipe-playing shepherds); the ground-floor hall ran back through the house, with a "powder room" under the stairs—a small mirrored plate around the light switch reflected the sight of my fingers as they approached the switch to turn it off. On the right as one came in through the front door was a room that doubled as cardroom and library. Beyond it down the hall was the large oak-paneled living room, where two big Chesterfield couches faced each other in front of the fireplace and two grand pianos reposed—one Steinway, one Baldwin, both in natural-finished wood. Next—up two steps and through a doorway—came the billiard room, with its wide-shouldered green-baize-covered table and, along one wall, shelves crammed with black-boxed phonograph records. Another door out of the billiard room brought one back into the hall at the rear of the house and past the breakfast room—a large alcove whose window let in daylight filtered by the maple trees in the backyard—and then to the back stairs and back door onto the driveway. By these stairs another corridor led farther back past a storeroom with a sink, sometimes used as a photographic darkroom, to the maid's quarters. Facing the other way at the foot of the back stairs, toward the front of the house, one entered the kitchen. This connected with the butler's pantry and, via a swing door, with the dining room. When I came down the back stairs my feet clattered on the uncarpeted treads. "*Walk*—don't run—Tony Bailey!" was a cry frequently heard.

In Britain, many children evacuated from deprived homes in large cities to the more comfortable provinces often found themselves at that time in startling conditions. Indeed, it's only recently that the term "all mod. con." (all modern conveniences) has come to be unnecessary in Britain when advertising flats and houses, as just about all dwellings come to have them. I wasn't unused to sanitation and hygiene, nor had I ever had to use an outside lavatory or boil water in a kettle for getting washed. But for a small English boy the amount of plumbing and hot water at 630 Runnymede, with its implications of almost limitless opportunities for scrubbing necks and poking washcloths into ears, might well have been horrifying. There were sinks, toilets, baths and showers everywhere one turned. For washing up *things* the butler's pantry had two small sinks, the kitchen a big one, the darkroom another. The powder room, chiefly for visitors, had a row of neatly monogrammed guest towels. Upstairs each bedroom had its own bathroom except at the back, where two bedrooms shared one. (There were six bedrooms on the second floor, and on the third floor, called "the attic" but hardly that, there were four more bedrooms plus two bathrooms and a playroom.) In the baths the water was prevented from escaping down the drain not with a simple rubber plug on the end of a chain, as in England, but by twisting a porcelain knob on top of a pipe, set in another pipe, so that it dropped into a water-blocking position. The incoming water was controlled by four large handles, each with four arms radiating from the center, and looking powerful enough for machinery at a waterworks, two at the top for the shower (another novelty for me), and the lower pair for the bath. In Britain at this time, members of the royal family were setting everyone a good example by putting only four inches or so of water in the tub, but at 630 we were allowed to have great depths. Making up for the necessity of getting washed, we could enjoy the miraculous floating property of Ivory soap and, almost, swim.

In many British homes (though not the Palace), water was heated, if at all, by individual "geysers," fired by gas, over the sink or bathtub. As you turned on the hot tap there would be a sudden whistle of gas, a bang and a blue flare (as the pilot light ignited the gas) that lit up the walls of the bathroom; hot water then began to fall in a skimpy stream. At 630, hot water cascaded in generous quantities from the appropriate taps—or faucets, as they were called in America. Only once was there a breakdown, which made me realize that our water came from the big coal-fired furnace in the basement, where it was tended by James; in addition, of course, the furnace provided heat for the radiators in every room in winter.

James also served at the dinner table and brought in drinks on a silver tray from his pantry. Drinks for "grown-ups" were not just sherry, whiskey and beer but highballs,

Manhattans, Old Fashioneds. However, James's main area of activity was the garage, which stuck out laterally from the rear of the house across the end of the wide concrete drive. Here were stored the screens and storm windows, which James put up and down with the passage of seasons. And here were kept the three cars: a gray La Salle convertible; a bright-red with varnished-oak trim Buick station wagon; and a black-and-gray Cadillac limousine. The La Salle had its spare wheel sitting in a dip of the running board, just in front of one of the doors. The Buick had three rows of shiny red leather seats. The Cadillac had velvety upholstery, a pair of tip-up seats that unfolded from the back of the front seat, and whitewall tires. James came to work in an upright Plymouth coupé and kept all of his charges splendidly gleaming. Tony Spaeth and I agreed that the La Salle was the best, though we liked sitting in the back seat of the Buick, and also pushing down the Cadillac's cigarette lighters and, when they popped up, looking at the red glow of the electric coils. "Automobiles" was another new word for me.

The house had many nooks and crannies, ideal for hide-and-seek, sardines and treasure hunts. At the head of the main staircase, over the front hall, was a wide landing, with a window over the front door, bench seats and built-in bookshelves. Here I sometimes stretched out for the afternoon nap that was compulsory during school vacations. Governesses and other authorities believed in divide-and-rule, and since a nap was more likely to be restful if TS and I were kept apart, I often managed to convince them that this spot—one of my favorites in the house—was all right for enforced siestas. There the afternoon sun packed with whiteness the muslin curtains—in summer they billowed in the warm breeze that came in through the half-open window. There, so that I wouldn't have to sleep, I stretched up an arm and plucked down from a bookshelf any volume whose title, binding or shape seemed interesting: a work by Stefan Zweig; *Lorna Doone;* a fat book called *Moby Dick.* To say that I read any of Melville's masterpiece would be inaccurate, but I turned its pages slowly, looking at words and lines and print, and dreamed in it, and I think some of it came through to me, in misty but indelible fragments.

In the attic there were further secret spaces, deep closets and cupboards under the eaves, filled with steamer trunks and hanging wardrobes. There, too, was the playroom, from whose dormer window we could look down over the gutter on James polishing the hood of the La Salle, parked in the driveway that was dark-patched with the sudsy water he had washed the car with. Up there among the Erector Set pieces, the model cars and trucks, was Tony Spaeth's prize toy, a six-foot-long wooden battleship, painted gray, something like a turn-of-the-century dreadnought, with an interior illuminated by a small bulb and a flashlight battery, and, on deck, a gun turret which revolved. Perhaps this large but not very realistic vessel was a link with Portsmouth and its great warships. At any rate, it did as much as anything else at 630 Runnymede to persuade me, in the first few days of my stay, that I had landed on my feet.

‖ 3 ‖

THERE WERE SEVERAL REASONS WHY THE SPAETHS DECIDED
to keep me and not any of the other nine children
whom Eloise Spaeth brought back to Dayton from the
Gould Foundation in New York. One was my name. Having two Tonys in one family was an interesting challenge.
Tony Spaeth's real name was Otto Lucien Anton Spaeth,
Jr., but to distinguish him from his father he had always
been called Tony. When practical problems arose from
having two Tonys (for example, giving us both a splendid
excuse for ignoring adult instructions—"Oh, I thought
you were calling *him* . . ."), Eloise Spaeth suggested I
might like to be called Anthony, but I declined, saying
I'd never been called anything but Tony. Therefore our
names were lengthened—their Tony became Tonyspaeth,
or Tony S., and I Tonybailey, or Tony B. If we were both
wanted at once, as for a meal or an errand, the short shout
"Both Tonys!" generally sufficed. Although she now had
four children, Eloise had lost a baby in the early thirties,
and had thought of starting an adoption agency. (Apart
from Tony, there were three girls: Marna, then fifteen;
Deborah, ten; and Mimi, another new arrival, four months
old.) The question of what I was to call Mr. and Mrs.
Spaeth also had to be settled—either Mom and Dad, falling
in with the Spaeth children, or Uncle Otto and Aunt
Eloise. I chose the latter, still feeling that I had a mother
and father.

A second reason I found myself with the Spaeths was
that the evacuation program that had brought me over

(and of which Eloise Spaeth was the coordinator for southwestern Ohio) required that children be placed in families
generally similar to their own. Religion was a major
factor. My mother was Catholic, and so—by baptism and
upbringing—was I. And so were the Spaeths. Two Jewish
girls were in the bunch Aunt Eloise brought to Dayton,
and she had a job finding a home for them. Jewish families in the right circumstances seemed to be in short supply.
But after a week or so at 630 the girls found a foster
mother in Miriam Rosenthal, a middle-aged unmarried
woman of great charm and resource, a public relations
agent and one of the mainstays of Dayton's musical life,
whom Eloise convinced of her duty to take in the Holder
sisters. On the same religious basis, the son of an im-
poverished Church of England vicar was billeted with a
very wealthy childless Episcopalian couple, the husband
being the chairman of a large industrial firm in Dayton,
and the lad—finding himself like me for the first time in
his life among butlers and cooks, with no other children
for company—mutinied; he refused to come home at night
from school and stayed with classmates; eventually another, less formal home was found, much to his host and
hostess' distress.

The foster parents whom Eloise Spaeth persuaded to
take out the necessary affidavits of support were by and
large very well off; most of the children came from professional middle-class British families that were not. So
some of the children were, in the terminology of the various children's welfare bureaus that kept an eye on us,
"overplaced"—misfits. (However, each of those Dayton
families really did want to look after a British child, as
did many in America at that time, and when the evacuation program came to an abrupt end, almost as soon as it
had started, with the sinking of a liner that had children
on board, Eloise had to rush to New York to collect her

quota before the supply dried up.) The fact that I was a Catholic and the Spaeths were the only Catholic volunteer sponsors brought us willy-nilly together. ("If you'd been a two-headed monster, we'd have had to take you," Eloise said later.) But Otto graciously used to claim a professional kinship with my father, then clerk-in-charge of the two-man branch of the National Provincial Bank in Portchester. Otto—in his first year out of an Illinois Franciscan college—had been a bank clerk too.

More than three quarters of a million unaccompanied children were evacuated within Britain in the first year of the war from the big cities to small provincial towns and the countryside. (Others went with mothers or aunts to what was hoped would be safe places.) But when, in the early summer of 1940, France fell and a German invasion of England seemed likely, there was a sudden rush to try to have children sent abroad. The government set up a Children's Overseas Reception Board, which received 211,000 applications in less than a month. On July 4 the authorities said the board couldn't handle any more applications, and on July 10 they suspended the program. They were alarmed by the rush to leave the country. They were also short of ships. When they suspended the program they were prompted by the loss of the *Arandora Star,* a fast unescorted liner; by the realization that it would be safer to send children on ships in convoys; and by (they said) the demands on the Admiralty to use most of the country's warships just then for anti-invasion duties —they couldn't spare them for escorting convoys. For a while, however, although the official program was shelved, it was possible for children to leave whose parents could send them privately, at their own risk.

My mother had read that spring in the *Daily Telegraph* of a plan apparently organized by the Boston *Transcript* (a newspaper, now defunct, that lives on in T. S.

Eliot's poem) for the evacuation to America of children
from "professional and clerical" families. She wrote for
information, mentioning the fact—which she hoped would
be influential—that she had once worked for the U.S.
Consulate in Southampton and knew several people in
America who would probably look after me if I was sent.
She received a reply a fortnight later from the London
office of the American Committee for the Evacuation of
Children. This committee—which had taken over, so she
gathered, the Boston *Transcript* scheme—had come into
being as a result of the efforts of people in New York who
were worried about the fate of European children as
Hitler's armies advanced. One of the committee's members was Mrs. Eleanor Roosevelt. While her husband was
trying to get across to Americans the idea that they too
would have to take on Hitler, and in the meantime was
aiding the British with old destroyers, Mrs. Roosevelt
helped set up this organization to bring British children
to the United States. The chairman of the committee thus
established was the Chicago newspaper publisher and
department-store heir, Marshall Field III. It acted with
promptness and perseverance, coming to grips with U.S.
government agencies, British officials, U.S. child welfare
organizations, the National War Fund and religious chari-
ties. By mid-July the committee had ferreted its way
through volumes of U.S. immigration law (much of it
designed to prevent the exploitation of foreign children
as cheap labor), and had persuaded the U.S. Attorney
General's office to rule that the committee could bring in
children who were unaccompanied and even unknown to
anyone in the United States. This was to be done through
a device known as a corporate affidavit. It allowed the
committee to guarantee the support of a specified number
of children between the ages of five and fifteen, and within
forty-eight hours after the affidavit was posted, receive the

required number of blank visas. These were sent to London to be filled in with the names of children waiting to leave for America—such as me.

I was in the garden at Edenholme, banging in stumps for an evening game of cricket with my father, when the question was put to me. My mother had heard from the London office of the committee that they would like to see me, naming a date in late July. Perhaps she had been in a dither all day, wondering how to put it to me, and, finally impatient to find out what I felt, came out to ask me just before my father got home from work. America? I said, at once, "Yes." I would like it. It would be an adventure. I had a dim notion that grandfather Bailey had been there as a cowboy when he was young—in Montana— and had brought back a saddle with silver decorations. America!

My father took me up on the train from Portsmouth, and we had a chance to see the defense preparations being made in earnest: anti-aircraft guns being sited; the glass roofs of the big stations being taped and painted over for blackout. Troops stood guard around a pile of metal— presumably a crashed plane—that lay on a village green. Our train was sent on several detours where bombs had fallen on the main line.

I had with me my birth certificate and ten photographs that would be needed if I was accepted for the plan. (While I was in Southampton with my mother having the photographs taken there was an air raid and we took shelter under the old Bargate—a remnant of the medieval walls of the city, pressing ourselves against the bumpy stonework of the gateway; it provided probably as good a shelter as there was to be found.) For me to take to London my mother had written down on a slip of paper our American "connections." For a start, there had been her job at the consulate in Southampton; then Roy Bower, my godfather, whose secretary she had been, and who was now American consul in Munich, Germany; and the names of various friends she had made who were back in America and might look after me. In any event, the committee decided they would take me on. The cost of passage, rail tickets and escort fees would be £24. My parents were warned to stand by for sudden word of a sailing. Two suitcases only would be allowed.

My "final advice" arrived on August 22. This took the form of a command to appear in the ballroom of the Grosvenor House Hotel in London on August 26, at 8 A.M. precisely, complete with suitcases, gas mask, passport, ticket and identity tags. My suitcases contained among other things a spare gray flannel suit, white flannels, rain-hat, three pairs of plimsolls (which I was soon to learn to call sneakers) and a pair of Wellington boots. The British tradition of being well if not always appropriately kitted-out for overseas travel was not being allowed to slip. But this departure was postponed without explanation, and the next word came by telegram stamped "Priority," ordering me to assemble at the Grosvenor House on September 16. In order to be there precisely at 8 A.M. my father and I caught a train up to London the afternoon before. Once again there were long delays while we were directed around repair works on the bombed track. One such excursion off the main line took us past a cricket match—green grass, white flannels, summer sunlight, the players seemingly rooted in England.

In London my father and I went to the Cumberland Hotel, at the Marble Arch end of Oxford Street, close to Hyde Park. The curtains of our room were closely drawn for the blackout. After something to eat, I went to bed with a copy of the *Hotspur* and immersed myself in a boys'-school adventure yarn while my father went down to the bar for a sorely needed pint of beer. Soon there was a distant thundery rumble; then, close-by, sirens that seemed to blare in surprise; and then, suddenly overlapping the sirens, a cracking, devastating roar that went on and on. I thought it was the end of the world. It seemed to approach me, getting louder and louder—the crack of doom; the earth must be caving in. I jumped out of bed and ran out into the corridor, past doors opening and people looking out. I was adding to the noise in the air outside. I shouted for my father, who, thank goodness, was coming up the stairs two at a time (the elevators had stopped). The noise? It was, he said, the anti-aircraft guns across the way in Hyde Park.

We spent the night in the basement dining room, along with the other guests of the hotel, on mattresses dragged down among the potted palms and cutlery sideboards and trolleys with little spirit stoves for crêpes and flambé sauces. Corridors or basements were thought to be safest, since they had no windows to be shattered into flying fragments of glass. It was a night typical of the first stage of the London Blitz, when some two hundred German bombers attacked the city every night. The next morning, after reporting to Grosvenor House, I was on my way with a group of other children to Liverpool. In Euston station we saw some captured German airmen under guard. I noted that the engine pulling our train was called The Welch Fusilier. We were several days in Liverpool, lodged in a school where we slept in long brick air-raid shelters. Then to the docks and the *Antonia*. She turned out to be the last ship to sail with children being evacuated. As my parents and indeed many in Britain were distressed to learn that week, a ship called the *City of Benares*—whose passengers included many children—was sunk by torpedo the day after we left London.

‖ 4 ‖

A FIVE-MINUTE WALK FROM WHERE I LIVE NOW, IN GREEN-wich, London, is the National Maritime Museum. Some-times, passing through it after a stroll in Greenwich Park, I find myself pausing by a glass-sided display case, in the section of the East Wing given over to Twentieth Century Marine Transportation, that contains a model (a little shorter than Tony Spaeth's wooden battleship but much more finely made) of a trim, two-funnel, twin-screw pas-senger and cargo vessel, painted in the rhubarb-red liv-ery of the City Line—the *City of Benares*. One's gaze can wander around the promenade deck and boat deck, count-ing the lifeboats in their davits. An accompanying placard gives the ship's specifications: length, beam, tonnage, date and place of construction, horsepower of the turbines, and details of the loss of life on September 17, 1940, when she was torpedoed after nightfall, in rough weather, 600 miles out from England. Among 406 passengers, 98 were English children aged between five and fifteen. Of the pas-sengers who survived, 13 were children. Some were killed at once by the explosion of the torpedo. Some drowned when lifeboats foundered. Others died of exposure before ships picked them up. In one lifeboat containing 40 adults and 6 small boys, the boys sang "Roll Out the Barrel" as the boat was lowered over the side. Then, missed by res-cue ships, they sailed eastward for eight days. Meals were half a biscuit and a fraction of sardine. Soon after food and water ran out, they were spotted by a flying boat; it radioed a warship, which rescued them.

The *City of Benares* was not the first ship to be sunk in World War II with children on board. The *Arandora Star* had gone down earlier, and on August 30 the Dutch liner *Volendam* was torpedoed off the north coast of Ireland with 320 children among the passengers. It was ten o'clock at night. The ship, hit twice, was listing badly when the order to abandon ship was given. Passengers and crew took to the boats and were picked up by other ships in the convoy. Unfortunately one small boy slept through the commotion, and when he woke up during the night it was to find his bunk at a funny angle and a strange silence everywhere in the ship. He went on deck, found the *Volendam* deserted and himself her only passenger; he returned to his cabin and fell asleep again. In the morning, when he went on deck again, he saw a destroyer standing by the still floating wreck. He waved, was seen and was rescued. The *Volendam* herself was towed to land and beached. But the *City of Benares* had much more impact as a disaster, and on October 3 the government program to send children overseas—for which applications had been suspended in July—was officially brought to an end. Some 600 children who were on their way to ships or had just embarked were returned to their homes. (The total figures for children evacuated overseas was 2,664 by the government and around 13,600 privately—including the 838 children sent by the U.S. committee, of whom I was one.)

Liverpool was being raided on the evening we left it. German bombers buzzed through loose cloud pockmarked by tiny dark ack-ack bursts. A bomb fell in the harbor close by the *Antonia*, sending cascades of Mersey water over one of the tugs that was chevying us out of dock. We wore life jackets and carried our gas masks in their little cardboard boxes on cords hung around our necks—tight-fitting rubbery masks to which were attached a sort of black cylindrical can with a filter in it. We were glad, once at sea, to be able to stow our gas masks in our cabins, though the bulky life jacket had to be carried around with us for the rest of the voyage. "Board of Trade—Child" it said on the jacket's scratchy orange canvas, filled with cork or kapok. We wore them at lifeboat drill, twice a day. We sat on them during morning singalongs on the poop deck, when the women who were escorting us led us in songs that spanned the Atlantic: "Swanee River" and "I Dream of Jeanie" from one side, "A Long Way to Tipperary" and "D'Ye Ken John Peel" from the other. Presumably this singing wasn't just energetic exercise for the lungs and larynx but was to take our minds off periscopes and torpedoes, and mummy and daddy. For a long time I thought one of the loveliest lines in English was "the sound of his horn in the morning." But I have it associated not with English hunting country, its views and deaths, but with the long gray Atlantic rollers, the neverending expanse of sea, and the gentle curve of the horizon broken by lines of ships, perhaps fifty of them in eight or nine columns, slow-moving, with tall plumes of smoke coming from the old coal-burning steamers among them —telltales which made more vital the zigzag course the convoy steered during the night. By the end of the year it was an ocean full of wreckage.

The *Antonia* had an old-fashioned, highly principled air about her. Erect and serious, with plumb stem and overhanging counter, a raised fo'c's'le and raised poop, and a skein of wires holding straight the lofty funnel with its Cunard White Star colors: black top and wide red bands divided by narrow black bands. The *Antonia*, said the company brochure, was one of Cunard's "popular 'A' liners" (others were the *Ansonia, Andania, Alaunia, Ascania* and *Aurania*) which in peacetime made the Liverpool–Montreal run, and offered cabin-class passengers

accommodations in what looked like comfortable bedrooms on shore. (There was no first class.) One of the
lounges was called the Long Gallery. "This room," said
the brochure, "with its oak panelling and restful indirect
lighting, has all the charm of a corner of some stately English country house."

We children were in tourist class, but now and then
moved in scavenging gangs through the stately restful corners. I wasn't seasick. Many of the adult passengers were,
including our escorts, and this gave us occasional freedom
to meander through the Promenade Bar on a rough evening, holding on to a table before making a sideways lunge
for a nearby chair, exaggerating the effects of lurch, pitch
and roll for the benefit of the stalwart drinkers, our exit
hastened by the shouts of the barman: "Get out of here,
you nippers!" On deck there was shuffleboard and quoits.
I saw an iceberg. An older boy told us cheerfully about the
Titanic. After five or six days the *Antonia* broke away from
the convoy during the night and sailed alone for Canada—
through fog on the Grand Banks, then down the wide,
green-banked St. Lawrence, where we were safe at last,
calling at Quebec, where for some reason U.S. Immigration examined and stamped our papers, then on to disem-
bark us at Montreal. In Montreal we ate huge quantities
of ice cream and heard a rumor that the ship which had
moved up to take our place in the convoy (destination
New York) had been sunk the day after we went off on our
own. The U.S. evacuation committee in London, having
received a cable from Canada, sent a printed postcard to
my parents informing them of my safe arrival. Joan
Hughes, the woman who had escorted me, wrote to my
parents when she got back to England to say that I had
behaved very well on the voyage but had (the two things
were apparently compatible) enjoyed myself thoroughly.

‖ 5 ‖

Tony Spaeth's gray battleship had been built by Tony's father, Otto, in his basement workshop, which was well equipped with power tools: band saw, rotary saw mounted in a table, miniature lathe and vertically mounted power drill. At the time of my arrival Otto was in the process of taking over a machine-tool factory in Dayton; he loved tools and gadgets of all kinds. New varieties of bottle openers and can openers, which he bought as they reached the stores, were constantly being tested by James and Artie, the cook. Otto had the first home-movie film camera in town, the first color film for it, the first electric typewriter, the first radio-controlled garage-door opener. Tony Spaeth and I were encouraged to shine our shoes more often than we would have done by the fact that once the polish was on, we could run into Otto's room and stick our shoes under his electric shoe buffer, which made one's toes tingle. The huge Capehart phonograph in the living room not only dropped a stack of 78-rpm records one by one onto the turntable but picked up each record, after one side was played, and turned it over, with various clicks and slithers, almost grunts and groans. When it went wrong, a man came all the way from Davenport, Iowa, to fix it. Otto's elder brother Bernard, who lived in Davenport, had recommended this repairman as an expert in Capeharts.

Otto himself was an inventor with the rare, canny gift of seeing the possibilities in other men's inventions, which he then sponsored, sometimes purely for his own pleasure. Much later, in a Wisconsin factory he owned, he kept a phonograph in his office whose needle arm lifted when the phone rang and returned to exactly the same place on the record when he replaced the receiver at the end of the call. One of his own ideas was a portable golf "caddie"—a light, tubular frame for carrying half a dozen clubs and balls, with a spike at the bottom for holding it upright in the ground when you put it down to play the ball. Another Otto idea was a double-ended thumbtack or drawing pin. The sight of a picture hanging crooked on a wall was a great annoyance to him, and with one end of Otto's thumbtack pushed into the plaster, the other firmly pressed into the back of the picture frame (set straight with the aid of a spirit level), no tilting was possible. Otto's first firm in Dayton was Dayton Type, Inc.; he was interested at that time in the invention of a malleable printing type, made in a sandwich of two alloys, one softer than the other, that when pressed firmly had enough "give" in it to justify a line—that is, enable the line to come out at the right length for the width of the column. Like many great inventions— the restrikable match, the perpetual electric light bulb— this type never went into production, though Otto sold the rights of it for a considerable sum to a large typefounding company. After Otto's death in 1969, Eloise received a letter from a man who wanted to express not only his sympathy but his gratitude. Otto, he said, had made his life by taking up and promoting his invention of a new improved garter for holding up men's socks.

As children, we didn't have much curiosity about the means by which Otto had reached his affluent position. He seemed to us very much *there*. However, we heard occasional references to his "first million," and also to "malt extract," which seemed to have been the foundation for the millions that followed. Otto's father had arrived in the United States from Bavaria in the 1870s, at the age of seventeen; he joined his brother, a priest, in Decatur,

Illinois, where there was a small German community, and
for three years worked as church organist and parochial-
school teacher in a back room of the small frame church.
Then he found a better-paying job as bookkeeper for the
local brewery and worked his way up to vice-president. It
was a typical American land-of-opportunity story, in Anton
Spaeth's case his success symbolized by a fine organ he had
installed in his home. Then came local prohibition. The
prosperous Decatur Brewing Company was driven to making a "temperance beer," then to bottling soft drinks; dis-
solution of the company was considered. But World War I
helped a little because rationed sugar supplies were in-
sufficient for the needs of bakery companies, and Frank
Schlaudeman, the brewery president and production man-
ager, invented a malt syrup that acted as both a sweetener
and fermenting agent.

Otto, one of seven children, had gone from his brief
banking career to a job as a car and tractor salesman in
Davenport, working with his brother Bernard. He then volunteered for the army, and was shipped off to Camp Pike,
Arkansas, for officer training. There—according to a story
with which he transfixed Tony Spaeth and me one day—
his most memorable experience was while out on maneu-
vers, when he encountered a tarantula "as big as my fist,"
and spent six hours lying petrified in fear it would jump
on him; eventually it stalked away. (In retrospect it is
hard to imagine Otto, despite his fear, having this sort of
patience.) The war ended before he was commissioned.
At this point he developed a chest infection, and wanting
to go to Colorado to recuperate, made money by selling the
Decatur malt syrup to bakers. This went well, and he continued as a malt-syrup salesman on his return from the
mountains with healthy lungs. However, the return of
plentiful sugar reduced sales; a new market was needed.
Prohibition was being approved in more and more states.

Otto was frequently asked, "Can you use that stuff for making beer?"

Thus the Decatur Brewing Company set up a subsidiary called Premier Products and began making Blue Ribbon malt extract for the specific purpose of selling it to those who wanted to brew their own beer. Otto was the salesman. He had read about modern sales techniques in *Printer's Ink*, the advertising journal, and in self-improvement manuals. He had natural flair and a conviction that communicated itself to listeners. He applied the experience he had gained in selling vehicles. He established a network of distributors across the country, and dreamed up advertisements geared to the locality. In St. Louis, with its big German population, ads depicted a plump German-American housewife, holding in one hand a good-looking home-baked loaf, in the other a can of Premier Products' malt syrup, and the slogan "Dot's vot Louie uses." Of course not saying vot he used it for, since everyone knew; and presumably all the Louies bought the syrup because it was what Hildegarde used too. Otto announced to the public: "With this malt extract a man will be able to make five gallons of good beer for $1.38, or if he wants more 'kick' in the beer, he can make three or four gallons for the same amount of money, depending entirely on the amount of water he uses."

In the twenties Blue Ribbon and Premier boomed; all over the country people made their own beer, as well as their own gin, wine and nameless hooch. Premier Products opened a new plant in Steubenville, Ohio, and took over two plants in Peoria, Illinois—one a former brewery, which was acquired for roughly the price the previous owners had spent on installing a sprinkler system. The company then merged with Pabst, which had been the nation's leading beer maker before Prohibition; and though this meant that other men were introduced into the leadership of the joint concern, Premier was much better placed than it otherwise would have been when Prohibition came to an end and beer could once again be bought legally. And thus Otto and other members of the Spaeth family had a considerable interest in the company, which as time went on dropped the name Premier and became known simply as Pabst (he and his brother Bernard were for many years the two largest single stockholders). Pabst was the beer Otto continued to drink all his life, loyal to the Blue Ribbon brand despite later ups and downs in the company's fortunes which had effects on his income. The names of Robert Pabst and of other executives of the company were often mentioned in conversations at 630 Runnymede between Otto and Eloise—conversations that weren't always cheerful, and that sometimes ended with Otto announcing that he was departing for Milwaukee to confer with Mr. Pabst and give him advice which, we gathered, Mr. Pabst was reluctant to take.

Otto never lost his interest in malt extract. In the 1950s he dallied with the idea of setting up a firm to make it again, and had a test survey conducted in a heavily German section of Pennsylvania-Dutch country to see what demand there was for it; but he took it no further.

He had had for a long time all sorts of other projects occupying him. The hometown boy—described by the Decatur *Herald and Review* as "affable and friendly, but perpetually dynamic"—married a hometown girl, Eloise O'Mara, and took her off to St. Louis to set up house. Then, in the mid-thirties, getting interested in printing, Otto decided to move to Dayton, Ohio. For an inventor-salesman-entrepreneur, Dayton was a worthwhile place. It was where Orville Wright, the aviation pioneer, still lived. (Wright was born in Dayton, and had, with his brother Wilbur, been involved in printing and a bicycle repair shop before they took to inventing planes.) Charles

Kettering, the inventor of the self-starter for automobile engines, was to be encountered on the golf course of Moraine Country Club, where Tony Spaeth and I now and then caddied for Otto. Dayton was famous at the turn of the century for its rolling-stock plants; at the time of Otto's arrival it was the home of many skilled craftsmen, who worked for small engineering firms and such large companies as General Motors, Frigidaire and National Cash Register. The livelihood of many others depended on the presence in the area of the two big adjacent air bases—Wright Field and Patterson Field.

Yet Otto's entry into the printing business was not particularly well timed. Dayton Type, Inc., was his company, and a Dayton resident named Peppelmeyer, inventor of a new linotype machine, was his current inventive protégé. But photo-offset printing was coming in. Eloise said later, "The war saved us." Otto, bailing out of printing, took over a company called Dayton Tool and Engineering, whose factory was in a converted tram shed on Lorain Avenue, on the east side of town. Dayton Tool worked overtime, turning out tools, dies, jigs, gauges and special machinery. Besides making tools, it mass-produced various items, including part of an ammunition-loading device for machine guns and part of an electric motor called a commutator. Dayton Tool won war-production honors. The Army and Navy "E" for Excellence flag flew from the factory flagpole, and decorated the company stationery. James drove Otto to Lorain Avenue at eight-thirty every morning, and generally brought him home by seven at night, in time to read or roughhouse with Tony S. and me for half an hour—perhaps a form of winding down, important for him and fun for us.

A number of the toys that were nominally given to Tony Spaeth and me were primarily Otto's playthings—though he needed us to help him enjoy them. Among the most

memorable were a five-foot-wingspan model plane, pow-
ered by a little gasoline engine and controlled by radio,
which Otto built, flew and crash-landed, and also an extensive model-railroad system in the basement, which
was out of bounds during construction and needed adult—
i.e., Otto's—hands on the controls thereafter. However, he
acquired his greatest toy a few years after the war. I saw
the plans and specifications on one return visit I made,
and saw photos later, but I unfortunately missed the thing
itself—a bus. In part it represented the customary ambi-
tion of a wealthy industrialist to own a yacht. Otto wanted
a yacht but he couldn't swim. After several months of wondering whether he should ignore this, and much reading of
yachting magazines trying to make up his mind whether
he should order one of the elegant craft built by Huckins
or Trumpy, Otto decided to stick with the land, which was
where all the golf courses were. He therefore bought a
thirty-five-foot Greyhound-type bus from General Motors,
without seats, and had Consolidated Ship Building Corporation on City Island, New York, fit it out as a land
yacht, with a master stateroom, two lavatories, and two
lounges, forward and rear, with couches that converted
into beds. A crew of two was hired, but this proved too
many, and so the roles of captain, engineer, deck hand and
steward were assumed by one man, a cheerful former truck-
driver named James Riley.

Otto's bus was soon nicknamed the Otto-bus or Spaethship; it prompted punny descriptions, such as Otto's
spaethious vehicle. It was painted in three shades of gray,
had curtains in the windows, and where a sign showing the
destination would have appeared in a normal bus was the
word PRIVATE. He kept the bus for three years, from 1948
to 1951, which was—for one of his enthusiasms—a long
time. The bus was a forerunner of all the Winnebagos,
Landcruisers and Mobile Motorhomes that have since

appeared, but in those days it was a novelty and attracted attention wherever it went. Otto and those members of the Spaeth family who had time to go along made extensive journeys in it; the bus visited or passed through forty of the then forty-eight states. Otto made business trips in it and used it for golfing holidays. He called on old friends and took distinguished persons for short hops. Otto admired Harry Truman immensely, and so called on the President at the White House to show him the bus. Tony Spaeth was at Millbrook School in New York State at this time, and Otto visited him there, much to Tony's initial embarrassment as the Spaethmobile rolled up to the school, though eventually he realized there was fame in having a father with a private vehicle like that. When Tony went on a tour of colleges, to see which he should apply for, he went with Otto in the bus. The bus's weight, eighteen and a half tons, was more than many highway bridges are presumably able to support, and reaching one of these, Otto and Riley would hold a conference and then proceed over it slowly. Otto developed a theory that bridges would bear twice their advertised weight limit. Otto of course had a radiotelephone on board. One acquaintance who spotted the bus cruising along Sunset Boulevard in Los Angeles was able to dash into a nearby drugstore, pick up the pay telephone, ask Information for Otto's call number and within a minute be talking to Otto. Naturally, Otto had Riley turn back and return to pick up the caller and take him for a spin.

The bus had a fitted galley with lights over the stove labeled "Turn and Bank Indicator," which Riley flashed when taking a bend while cooking was being done under way, but it generally stopped for meals at diners and restaurants. However, Otto often took the opportunity to dine on some of his favorite foods: canned black-bean soup, pumpernickel bread, and Le Sueur peas, which he ate cold, straight from a dish into which they had been decanted, with a sprinkling of black pepper and a dash of Tabasco sauce. On one occasion the bus stopped at a restaurant for Eloise to have dinner, while Otto stayed on board for such a snack. Afterward he told Riley to drive on. Forty minutes later Eloise called him on the telephone to remind him that she wasn't on board but was still at the restaurant, waiting for him to drive back and pick her up.

‖ 6 ‖

DURING MEALS AT 630 RUNNYMEDE DRIVE THE HABITS, LIKES and dislikes of a seven-year-old English child met the customs and attitudes of Otto and Eloise Spaeth. The points of encounter were sometimes painful. Breakfasts, taken in the breakfast room with the other children and the current governess, were no great difficulty, although for one who had been used to the rough, more demanding properties of porridge oats, cooked for an hour or so the night before and warmed up the next morning, such smooth hot cereals as Wheatena and Cream of Rice seemed like baby food. Other novelties like French toast, grits and waffles found rapid acceptance; maple syrup was wonderful. Moreover, what the Americans affably called English muffins struck me as a great improvement on any home-grown English product, whether muffins or crumpets of the kind I'd been used to—it was a pity only that there was no real marmalade to put on them. I hated the condensed agricultural taste of V-8 juice, but otherwise welcomed American efforts to distribute vitamin C by way of orange juice and grapefruit juice, in generous quantities. American milk, served in tall tumblers—sometimes former peanut-butter jars with transfers of cartoon characters on them—was at first daunting and tasted "different," but I was soon downing a quart a day without trouble.

At the Gould Foundation in the Bronx we had been introduced to hamburgers. While in New York, we went on trips to the World's Fair and Yankee Stadium, and discovered hot dogs and popcorn. Cracker Jack and Tootsie Rolls made up for any distress caused by being far from English sweet shops that sold vast varieties of candy, including my favorite liquorice allsorts and mint humbugs. Twenty-five cents a week pocket money gave us the wherewithal for a pack of Juicy Fruit gum, a bar of Baby Ruth chocolate, and a roll of caps, which I used in a toy .38 automatic, stamped "Special Detective," that I had acquired in New York. At seven, two of the great pleasures are to have sweet things in the mouth and be able to make loud bangs. For lunch at the Spaeths' we generally ate soup and a sandwich: peanut butter and jelly or a BLT (bacon, lettuce and tomato), which, with lots of mayonnaise, on rye bread, remains for me one of the indigenous glories of American cuisine. But dinners—meals often taken formally with Otto and Eloise in the dining room—could be a problem.

We stood behind our chairs. Tony Spaeth or I, whoever was closer, was expected to step over and pull out Eloise's chair for her and push it in under her; then we sat down. Otto began grace—"For what we are about to receive . . ." —and we joined in. After that we could unfold our napkins. The table—long, with slightly rounded ends—was gleaming mahogany. Knives, forks and spoons of different shapes and sizes paraded on each side of the mat, and a tall goblet stood ready to receive milk or iced water; a finger bowl, whose purpose was at first mysterious to me, presented a surface on which the light of table candles or the candle-shaped wall-bracket lights shimmered. Several large oil paintings on the walls formed a backdrop on which one's eyes could rest, not with the intention of looking at the pictures but of seeking relief from the business at hand, which required concentration and even courage.

James brought in the first course at the summons of an electric buzzer, placed on the floor by Eloise's right foot. He came in from the butler's pantry, through a door

hinged so that it could swing both ways, and with a port-
hole through which the person pushing it could see that no
one was coming the other way. I had no experience of butlers—hadn't seen them in plays or read about them in novels, and the sight of James with the silver soup tureen or
the platter of stuffed avocados was stirring: James in white
jacket and black tie, bent slightly forward from the waist,
not speaking but giving his attention to holding the dish
at just the right point in space so that the hand, arm and
plate of the person being served were brought into appropriate conjunction. His skill and natural correctness deserved emulation. Our manners were indeed expected to
be first-rate: the cutlery properly employed; no talking
with food in the mouth; sitting up straight without elbows
on the table, and any hand that was not employed with
knife, fork or spoon lying still, a symbol of rectitude, in
one's lap. I, being English, was allowed for the time being
to go on holding both knife and fork in, respectively, my
right and left hands. But it was explained to me, when
I looked askance at the Spaeth way—the knife being held
only during the operation of cutting, then put down and
the fork transferred to the right hand—that this was the
American fashion. A small piece of bread could be used
as a "pusher" to assist errant scraps of food, such as peas,
onto the fork. Otto gave this custom a provenance, as he
often did with things—a reason, some historical background. He said that it had been introduced here by
German-Americans—had come about originally at the
court of a Prussian king who had lost an arm and had been
forced to use knife and fork alternately in the same hand,
and was thus—to make him feel better about it—copied
by his subjects. (This story, impressive at the time and
illustrative of German willingness to pamper the disabili-
ties of their leaders, now seems less likely to be true. I
wonder if the habit may be explained as arising from

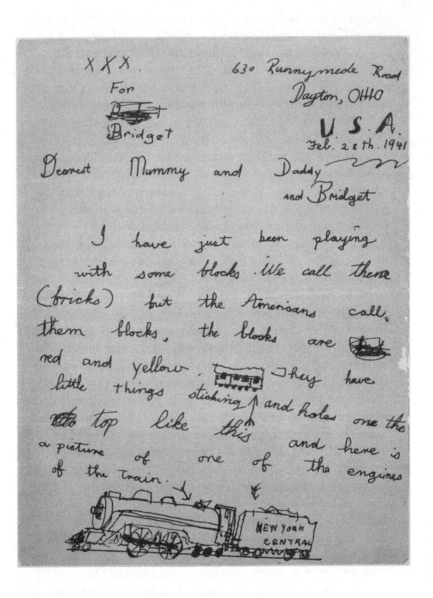

XXX.
For
~~Bridget~~
Bridget

630 Runnymede Road
Dayton, OHIO
U.S.A.
Feb. 2 6 th. 1941

Dearest Mummy and Daddy
and Bridget

I have just been playing
with some blocks. We call them
(bricks) but the Americans call
them blocks, the blocks are
red and yellow. They have
little things sticking and holes on the
top like this and here is
a picture of one of the engines
of the train.

NEW YORK
CENTRAL

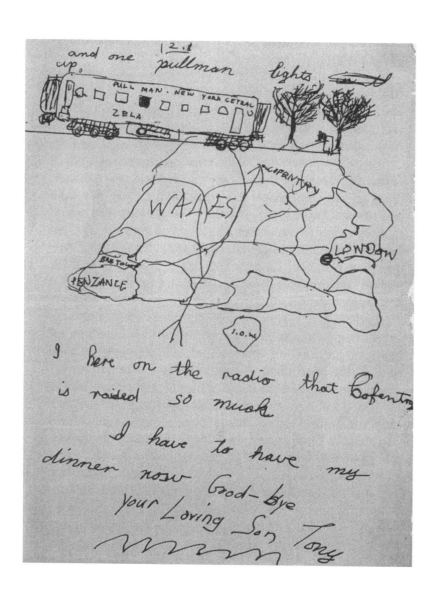

I here on the radio that Cofentry
is raided so much

I have to have my
dinner now Good-bye
your Loving Son Tony

pioneer conditions, where a fork was a luxury, and a knife often had to serve both for cutting food and lifting it to the mouth.)

None of the Spaeth etiquette might have been insuperable by itself, but taken together with adult-inspired and, to me, foreign food, obstacles arose. I disliked—in fact, couldn't stand the taste of—most vegetables whose names began with *a*. That meant asparagus, aubergine, artichoke, and avocado. I also hated okra, spinach and all forms of squash, and I didn't much like sweet potato. But the rule was: Finish your vegetables or you won't get any dessert. And unless the dessert was pumpkin pie, which I didn't much like either, that could be a tragic loss: devil's food cake, chocolate cake, angel food cake, blueberry cheese cake, fudge ripple ice cream . . . And so, before reaching the paradise of Artie's desserts, one had to trudge through the purgatory of vegetables. I had my fingers crossed as James ceremonially paraded them into the dining room, doubly crossed as the lid was taken off the dish, and my feet crossed for good measure as Eloise said, "Pass your plate, Tonybailey"—for the serving of vegetables was judged too crucial a task to be delegated to children—and I watched anxiously the size of the helping that was being heaped on my plate. Green and slippery and snakelike was asparagus. Slimy, with nasty little seeds, and a ghastly color, was eggplant. Spinach, piled in a dark-green mound, looked like a clump of undergrowth one might come across in a dark forest inhabited by bats, bandits and witches, with monsters ready to crawl out of it; it would taste of stagnant pools and putrid vegetation. I almost gagged on my first bite of it. I tried taking surreptitious gulps of milk or water to wash it down. This sometimes caused, rather than cured, chokes and coughs. I tried spreading it around my plate, hiding a little under a piece of pork rind or a fragment of baked potato skin (a great sacrifice, since I liked baked potato skin). I tried not to watch Tony Spaeth, who would be adopting similar ruses; seeing me looking at him, he might break into a giggling fit. Often there were lectures addressed to one or the other of us about the need to eat vegetables and how good they were. Encouragements were tried, firm words and, ultimately, ultimatums. "Either you eat up or . . ." I closed my eyes, hoping that the reduction of one sense would diminish the other, so that the poisonous, icky stuff would pass through my mouth and down my throat untasted.

Tony Spaeth often had problems more intense than I. Not only did he not like many of the vegetables but he was frequently accused of bad manners while trying to eat them. Thus for punishment and rehabilitation he would be made to stand in front of the tall, four-paneled mirrored screen next to the swing door of the butler's pantry, there to watch himself—with lips tightly compressed, as ordered—munching a mouthful of, say, summer squash. I, sitting at that end of the table on Otto's left hand, would attempt to avoid meeting Tony's eyes reflected in the mirrors—eyes that might be filled with humiliated tears or with a tremendous sense of the comedy inherent in the occasion. James at these times would march into the room, tray in hand, looking as if it were an effort for him to keep a straight face as he passed the screen and its captive, and Eloise would declare, "Only five dishes for dessert, James —Tonyspaeth is not having any."

ONE of the few ways in which Otto's German background manifested itself was in food. There were weekly trips to a German bakery in downtown Dayton for rye bread and black bread. Later, in New York, he regularly ate at restaurants like Lüchow's and Forester's where he could get such dishes as corned beef and cabbage, sauerbraten and potato dumplings. On farmland which he rented outside

Dayton for his factory employees to grow vegetables for victory, Otto grew (I believe by proxy) cabbages; his crop was bottled in several hundred Mason jars as sauerkraut. He was not a heavy eater, and when I was tucking away a second helping of meat and potatoes ("No, no more broccoli, thank you, Aunt Eloise"), Otto filled in the odd spots with a side dish of rye bread and gravy. Every night he also had a bowl of Hungarian green peppers. This delicacy—pickled, looking like wrinkled and twisted green prunes—was one of the hottest take-the-skin-off-the-roof-of-your-mouth edibles known to man, and Otto claimed it kept him in good health; he never had a cold. There was a period of crisis, late in the war, when no Hungarian green peppers were to be had, and there was talk of trying to grow them on the victory farm. But he found a new source before long, and before the cold germs found a way through his defenses.

Rationing seemed to have little effect on dining at 630 Runnymede. At least I wasn't conscious of any real shortages, though there were apprehensions of some in 1943, when sugar, coffee and meat were all rationed, and the local weekly paper, the *Oakwood Press*, headlined an editorial "FAMINE LOOMS IN AMERICA." Trial blackouts had been conducted by then, and we were participating in the war effort by saving tin cans—taking their labels off, flattening them and putting them by the curbside for collection. Waste fat and grease were taken to butcher shops and sent off to be made into glycerine, for explosives. Gas rationing was a year old, and long-distance callers were advised to be brief—"The War needs the wires." I yearned for a shortage of asparagus and artichokes.

Otto and Eloise had breakfast in their bedrooms. Identical round silver trays went upstairs, each with a silver coffee pot, a grapefruit and a slice of toast. Otto and Eloise had similar suites of rooms—bedroom, dressing room and bathroom—Otto's at the front and Eloise's at the back of the house, and connected with each other by way of the upstairs screen porch, where in summer they sometimes breakfasted together. When Otto's breakfast tray was brought back down in the morning it was accompanied by another tray on which stood two or three empty blue-labeled bottles of Pabst; he took beer up nightly to help him sleep.

|| 7 ||

A TELEGRAM HAD GONE OFF TO MY PARENTS FROM THE
Spaeths, announcing my arrival in Dayton. Letters followed. Some confusion had resulted from the fact that
when my mother's old friends Mr. and Mrs. Justin Fuller
of Washington, D.C., heard that I was on my way into the
unknown, they had called the evacuation committee's
New York headquarters and put in a bid for me; but they
somehow hadn't registered this request with the right person, or in the right way. Miffed, they wrote to my godfather, Roy Bower, who was temporarily away from his
Munich post and in Switzerland. He took one of their remarks to mean that my situation was unsatisfactory or
problematical and fired off a godfatherly cable to the committee, asking what was up. The committee, believing
there was a move to remove me from the Spaeths, did
some hasty checking around. My parents, the Spaeths and
various social agencies were consulted. Everyone decided
I was in the best of hands. Letters of appeasement were sent
to the Fullers and Roy Bower. My parents expressed the
hope that the Spaeths hadn't taken all this the wrong way;
they were immensely grateful to them for having taken me
in. A caseworker from the Catholic Children's Welfare
Agency who dropped by the Spaeth household at Christmas
got the absolutely accurate impression that I couldn't have
been in better circumstances, and wrote to my parents to
say so.

The Spaeths gave a party that first Christmas for the
Dayton English children, and photographs of us were

taken standing and kneeling around the tree, the silver
wings of whose crowning angel brushed the ceiling of the
living room, and the dark-green branches of which—
laden with fragile decorations and lit by twinkling white
lights—overhung a great pile of beautifully wrapped presents. At home I had had to wait until Christmas morning
for certainty that there was to be anything, when I woke
to find a pillowcase with presents in it lying at the foot of
my bed. In Dayton the catalog of the F. A. O. Schwarz toy
store in New York was an early December harbinger of
things to come. Then, on Christmas Eve, not long after
Tony Spaeth and I had been bundled off to bed, the house
was filled with the sound of bells—sleigh bells, it had to be
explained to me. And presently, up the stairs clomped the
red-suited, white-bearded man, brushing snow off his
shoulders, going "Ho ho ho" and demanding of TS and
me whether we were good boys and what we hoped Santa
Claus would bring us. My final fragments of belief in
good St. Nicholas were here held together by the strangeness of the event to me, the acceptance by TS and his
family that it was all perfectly normal, the weird name
Santa Claus (unlike our prosaic English Father Christmas) and the sense of promise the jovial fellow radiated.
I fell asleep unsure if I had awakened from a dream, but
sure that if it had been a dream, the gifts implicit in the
visitation would be real.

One letter my mother received at this time came from a
Dayton woman, Mrs. Jay Leach, who had read about my
arrival in a local paper. Considerately putting herself in
my mother's shoes, she thought my mother would like to
know something about my general surroundings. Dayton,
she wrote,

> is an inland manufacturing city with a population of two
> hundred and twenty thousand. We have good schools,

plenty of churches and lovely homes. The climate is change-
able. Usually very warm summers and cold winters, but our
houses are heated. I added that last because I remember
one winter years ago I spent in London and at that time a
heated house was hard to find.

I feel sure that all the children here will be given the
best of care. We all so sympathize with you parents, that
we are eager to give you every assurance that all will be well,
especially with the small lad so far from you.

The small lad also wrote, succinctly:

Dear Mummy and Daddy. I hope you are well. I hope
Bridget has a very Happy Birthday. I have just come home
from school. I am very happy over here. I hope the Clipper
on which I am sending this letter does not fall to the
Germans.

Much love from your loving son
Tony

Eloise, and occasionally Otto, wrote as well and told my
parents how I was growing, eating, putting on weight and
getting on at school. I was supposed to write home once a
week; sometimes I had to be reminded, or prodded with
the suggestion that I should come into Eloise's room so
that she could see that the letter got written. There I lay
on the carpeted floor, using her crinkly onionskin air-mail
stationery with a red printed line up one side and a blue
line across the bottom, apparently fencing in on the paper
my energetic scrawl. But how slowly the words sometimes
came. I bit the eraser end of my pencil between useful
thoughts. I allowed myself to be distracted by young Mimi
in her playpen but got some copy out of it by recording
the news that she had just dropped her doll over the side
or was trying to stand on her head. I must have missed
my three-year-old sister. Xs as kisses decorated the borders

of my letters, and many were inscribed as specifically for Bridget. "Dear Bridget," went one footnote addressed to her, "I wish you were here but then there would be no one to stay with Mummy and Daddy." My mother must have taken heart from some things I wrote, and perhaps grieved at others—for example, the first letter in which, not long after my arrival in Dayton, I switched from "Dear Mummy" to "Dear Mother." Once in a while "Your loving son" was replaced by "So long."

My letters home contained random pieces of wartime information that didn't seem to bother the censors. "I have sixteen pictures pasted on the wall of my room— one is of the British raiding the Lofoten Islands in Norway." "I hear the Germans have a dreadful new four-engined bomber." "I am glad to hear the British are beating the Italians." "I hear on the radio that Coventry is raided so much. The French were brave to sink their own ships at Toulon." Was all this sympathy conventional, or did I have a youthful glimmering of what it was like, below those dreadful bombers, in Coventry, or for French sailors opening the seacocks and placing explosive charges in their own ships? I remembered to mention to my parents when parcels or photographs arrived or when they failed to turn up as promised. Once, at Eloise's suggestion, I enclosed a teabag in one of my letters. I never admitted or even suggested that I missed my parents or felt homesick, though on one occasion, after mentioning the school play that I was in, I said: "It would be nice if you were here to see it." A word now and then indicated that I still realized which was my real home—for instance, "P.S. Please put the stamps on this envelope in my stamp album." I often expressed a hope that my father would serve in the navy, but when he became an army officer I wrote proudly: "I am very glad—maybe you can someday come back with the Victoria Cross"—not knowing, it seems, that

most Victoria crosses were awarded posthumously. I listed
new toys: roller skates, ice skates, an air rifle, a combined
pen-pencil ("It cost 25 cents and I bought it with my own
money"). "Here is a picture of my big clockwork Thunderbolt racing car." I gave short accounts of the plots of
films we saw, like Sabu's *Elephant Boy, Bambi's Children*
and *Passage to Marseilles,* and described new books I'd
been given, on Benjamin Franklin and Scott of the Ant-
arctic. "At school I got all the ribbons and the prize which
means that I was the hardest worker in our room."

The verb "got" in that boast was an early touch of
Americanization. Soon I was writing "I had a fine time
Easter," dropping the "at" that would have been necessary in England. Sometimes I remembered that my parents
might be ignorant of American customs: "Halloween
means lots of people dress up and play jokes. I am going
to dress up as a ghost." An Erector Set, I explained, was
the American version of Meccano. My parents sent me the
Meccano magazine throughout, and it came in fits and
starts. Some of my letters took four weeks or more—my
mother noted on a few of them: "Received six weeks
later" or "We received this letter as we were all at Xmas
Day dinner." (She didn't explain how the post came to be
delivered on Christmas Day.) Air mail, by "Clipper,"
didn't necessarily help—Eloise said air mail went via Ber-
muda, where the censors kept it a long time. Some letters
sent by sea arrived damp and salt-stained. Some never
arrived.

‖ 8 ‖

As my father and I stood on the turfed-over roof of our air-raid shelter in the late summer of 1940, we watched the first aerial attacks on Portsmouth and Southampton. Black smoky bursts of anti-aircraft fire drifted across the sky. There would be a sudden orange flare as aircraft machine-gun bullets hit one of the barrage balloons, tethered high over the docks at the ends of wire cables, and which surely attracted raiders rather than keeping them away from the interesting targets below. From our distance, ten miles or so from each of the ports, it was like a fireworks display at which I could ooh and aah. But we were ready to forgo the spectacle and duck into the shelter if the Jerries over Portsmouth headed westward, and the sirens sounded in turn in Fareham, Titchfield and Park Gate. The shelter was the shape of a slightly elongated igloo, its low doorway partly protected from blast by an earthwall placed athwart the threshold. Inside, it was cramped, and damp, and gave one uncomfortable feelings of being already in a tomb.

On my Park Gate bedroom wall, in addition to posters showing all the classes of ship of the Royal Navy, I had put up identification charts of British and German planes, but the sky over the ports was, as my father had intended by moving us there, generally at a safe distance. It was hard to tell whether those vapor trails were being made by Heinkels or Dorniers. And sailing out of Liverpool, I saw no recognizable sources for the bombs, falling out of the tormented night sky, that nearly capsized the *An-*

tonia's tug. The enemy remained anonymous. But some planes were apparent. As I prepared to leave for America, the small wood-working factory down Duncan Road from our house, where panniers and punnets were manufactured for the local strawberry crop, was being converted to take on the repair of battle-damaged Spitfire and Hurricane wings. The wings arrived, separated from their fuselages, on flatbed railway wagons at Swanwick station, a little farther down the road. My family connection with the air was by way of my mother's youngest brother, Patrick Molony, who had been a member of the works team at Supermarine in Southampton, builders of the Schneider Trophy–winning seaplane, the immediate ancestor of the Spitfire—which Supermarine went on to build. Among my Dinky Toy models (H.M.S. *Hood,* a London double-decker bus and a rubbish lorry) were the planes I played with most: an Imperial Airways Vickers; an Avro Anson (a dowdy two-seater); and both a Spitfire and a Hawker Hurricane, the two fighter planes that went up and down in my favor. The difference between those similar-sized machines was puzzling—perhaps it was one simply of style. The Spitfire appeared more sprightly and debonair; the Hurricane had an earnest, reliable look.

I used to draw them at home and at school, locked in combat with Messerschmitts and Junkers, and I went on drawing them in Dayton—though as time went on, they were joined by other aircraft in the sketches that filled up some of the yawning, wordless spaces in my letters home. In the margin of a page with two dozen words written on it in my splashy round script I would draw a plane hurtling toward the kisses at the bottom; my caption explained: "New U.S. fighter goes 725 mph in a dive." Beneath my signature I would draw a scene showing my father shooting down Nazi planes with a revolver and afterward receiving a medal. But gradually my aircraft lost the dapper Spitfire look and acquired the stubbier, broader-shouldered American stance, partly resulting from the radial rather than in-line engines that marked some of the creations of Grumman and Curtiss, and which I liked drawing, with big, pointed propeller bosses protruding from the radiator cowlings like the knobs in the centers of Viking shields. I drew whole pages of planes under such written legends as "Keep 'em Flying," "Happy Landings" or, with a German plane spinning downward, "Keep 'em Falling." Bell Airacobra, Brewster Buffalo, Chance-Vought Corsair, Boulton-Paul Defiant . . . I thought planes, loved planes and certainly wouldn't have believed anyone who said that, as with girls who were soppy about horses, it was just a phase.

While it lasted the passion simplified present-giving. One Christmas, Otto gave me a *Complete Book of Planes.* Several Biggles books came from England, the airborne adventures of the redoubtable British ace enhancing my own daydreams of being at the controls of a Bristol Blenheim on a secret mission over Europe or a Martin Marauder over Pacific islands. It was a treat to go to the movies, but even more of one to go to *Eagle Squadron, Flying Tigers* or *A Yank in the R.A.F.* Our heroes were "aces," like Captain Joe Foss, of the U.S. Marine Corps, who had shot down twenty-six Jap planes. I was given a set of stationery with the letterhead "United States Army Air Forces" under the USAF insignia of wings crossed by a propeller. Tony Spaeth had the U.S. Coast Guard motif on his writing paper, poor fellow.

Although Dayton was an "inland manufacturing city," it was the perfect place for a plane-lover. Dayton residents were quietly proud of the fact that Orville Wright still lived in Oakwood, two blocks away from 630 Runnymede, in a huge Greek Revival–style house. And though he had a reputation as a recluse—he hadn't flown since 1918—

Otto once or twice went to visit him and was allowed to see the garage-workshop where Wright continued to putter. (In 1940 Wright was sixty-nine. When President Roosevelt came to Dayton that fall, campaigning for the presidential election, he got Wright to drive with him around town in an open car, but as they reached the corner of Far Hills Avenue and Park Avenue, by Oakwood City Hall, Wright asked the driver to pull up. He bade a curt farewell to the President and got out, saying, "I can walk home from here.") The two big air bases, named after the Wright brothers and John Patterson, founder of Dayton's leading industry, National Cash Register, were a few miles out of town to the northeast, and Otto's position as a leading defense contractor took him to them frequently. On display days he took Tony S. and me to see planes like the new B-17 Flying Fortress, with its impressive gun turrets bulging on all sides, and the weird Northrop Flying Wing, which looked like a child's invention. Distinguished aviators came to dinner at the Spaeth house. Sir Richard Fairey, the British manufacturer of naval aircraft (Fairey Fulmar, Fairey Firefly, etc.), stayed for several days, and Otto took him over to meet Orville Wright. Eventually two of the rarely used attic bedrooms were inhabited by two air force officers, one from Australia, one from New Zealand. They were working at Wright-Patterson (as the twin fields came to be called), and I appreciated their presence not so much from Commonwealth pride as because they gave me a dime-a-week contract for keeping their shoes polished.

I spent much of my earnings at this time on kits and materials for model planes. Hours were spent shaping balsawood and trying to get the tissue paper (doped to stick to the wood) to look like smooth wing fabric or metal fuselage covering and not a wrinkly, corrugated mess. The results weren't always a satisfactory resemblance to the model pictured on the box. One Hawker Hurricane kit ended up as a plane that looked (I wrote to England) "something between a Hurricane and a Grumman Wildcat." The models were flimsy, easily damaged in test flights or dogfights with Tony Spaeth's air force. A Focke-Wulf 190 on which I had labored long and for which I developed profoundly affectionate feelings—its clean, functional design and vivid light-green color making me set aside any antipathy held because of its enemy origins, even as I stuck to the wings the black Luftwaffe crosses—did not survive many days in active service. I decided to give it a fitting funeral by sending it down in flames from the window of the attic playroom. Tony Spaeth stood by, making rat-a-tat-tat anti-aircraft gun noises as I lit the match. This I touched to one green tissue-papered wing and thrust the plane out over the eaves. It glided briefly, flames spreading fast, and then—to the sounds of our cheering—fell cartwheeling toward the driveway below.

An angry shout came from down there. TS and I chanced a quick look out over the roof edge and saw James, standing by the open hood of the Cadillac, blowing on his fingers—singed, it was immediately clear, in plucking the blazing fighter plane from its landing place on top of the car's twelve-cylinder engine. James had a stern word with me when I went down to face him, but he didn't tell.

|| 9 ||

DESPITE THE MISCHIEVOUS ASPECTS OF THAT INCIDENT, I wasn't often in trouble. In fact, I've sometimes wondered whether the effect of those Dayton years was to make me a more law-abiding small boy than I might otherwise have been. It was difficult to be bad when you were a guest in someone's house—though according to evacuation tales in England, later embodied in novels by Joyce Cary and Evelyn Waugh, not every evacuated child felt this way. I was conscious of my role as an ambassador. Whether because of wartime patriotism or the Portsmouth naval tradition, perhaps transmitted in a school history lesson, I had taken to heart Nelson's flag signal, flown on the *Victory* before the battle at Trafalgar, "England expects every man to do his duty." "Tony Bailey has delightful manners," people said to the Spaeths, or wrote in similar strains to my parents. "Conduct: excellent," it said in my school reports.

Although I ran into the usual adult flack for slamming doors or shouting to Tony Spaeth from one end of the house to the other, it was generally Tony S.—perhaps seeking a share of the limelight I had unfairly attracted— who was the first to get into hot water. Otto (I learned later) wrote to my father at one point saying that he occasionally had to be a little harder on me than I deserved because he feared that otherwise Tony Spaeth would be impossibly jealous. There were a couple of strict house rules: no playing on the billiard table, which we had damaged twice; and no talking in bed once the lights had been turned off. Tony Spaeth was quite incapable of *not* talking in bed—I was eventually moved into another room so that we could get some sleep. But while we shared a room and a pair of maple bunk beds, he (and I) went on talking. Most nights there would be two or three warnings, delivered by Miss Sjolin or Eloise: *"No more talking!"* Then, finally, a command would come to report downstairs to the kitchen, where Otto awaited us. A short speech was made to the convicted; then summary punishment—quickly over Otto's knee and a hard spank or two with the hand. In preparation for that brief instant of pain I tried to keep my gaze on some object—the electric clock; the door handles or impressive hinges of the big monitor-top refrigerator. Miss Sjolin, if called upon to administer justice, preferred a hairbrush. She walloped us in turn with the back of it on one occasion when Tony S. and I had been playing on the garage roof (forbidden territory, but accessible via a tree in the backyard), and we had ignored—she said—her calls to us to come down. We claimed that we hadn't heard her.

Perhaps there had been distant sounds which—if we'd wanted to—we could have identified as coming from Miss Sjolin. Grownups are quick to accuse children of disobedience, when in fact children may simply not be tuned in to the wavelength of volition that makes possible a choice between obedience and disobedience. Instead, they are involved in themselves. My one serious conflict with Otto occurred in this manner, and I retained for a long time a sense of injury; my honor had been impugned. But now, so much later, I'm not sure. Perhaps I really had been in the wrong, and the conveniently turned-down rheostat of a child's conscience and attention had refused to let through the correct, and justified, charge.

The circumstances of the case were these. Otto was building (for Tony Spaeth and me, he said) something in the cellar. It was going to be for Christmas. That much we were told because there was no way of disguising the quantities of timber being taken down there or the craftsmen who went down for one reason or another. TS and I were asked to give our word that we would stay out of the cellar, and did so. One December afternoon just after we had got home from school a man came to the back door. He said he was a mason, come to knock some holes in a cellar wall, and could I show him where to go. I didn't think. I set off ahead of him down the cellar stairs and turned left, opening the door of Otto's workroom for him and turning on the light. I pointed ahead into the two rooms beyond and said, "In there." I went no farther, glimpsing a mass of wood shavings, newly built benches, wires and not much else, before dashing back up again.

I truly believed I hadn't broken my promise. When Otto confronted me in the billiard room that evening, tipped off somehow, perhaps by the mason, it came as a great surprise to me.

"Did you go into the basement, Tony?" he said.

"Well, no, not really," I replied.

Otto asked again, "Did you go into the basement?"

And once again I said "No," and might have gone on to mumble an explanation, how I hadn't really seen anything that would spoil his surprise for us, how the mason hadn't known where to go, when Otto slapped me on the cheek.

"You mustn't lie," he said. "You must keep your word."

I nodded my agreement, suddenly wet-eyed and hot-faced—but aware, too, that things were not quite as simple as he believed.

The model railroad in the basement was a success for Otto, despite our little drama. It was unveiled on Christmas morning. The tracks ran on several levels through two rooms. Trains came through the walls and ran along trestles and embankments and over bridges and through tunnels. There was a small town, with factories and a marshaling yard, where freight cars could be shunted and spare rolling stock stored. The passenger trains, pulled by a diesel engine, were in Pennsylvania Railroad colors, but the freight cars were generally pulled by a black Pacific-type steam locomotive of the Chesapeake & Ohio. There were frequent problems with transformers, switches and fuses that shut down the system for several days at a time while electricians searched for short circuits. Tony S. and I admired the way the headlights beamed from the loco-motives as we ran them in the dark, and the bells rang at grade crossings, the gates lowering across the roadways, before the trains passed. But it was mostly Otto's play-thing, at least until he got bored with it. It was too com-plete for children. TS and I preferred games with only a few fixed or given elements so that we had more room to pretend.

My good behavior eventually had to be disowned. At the age of eighteen I found myself in the British army, on two years' national service, standing before a fierce-looking colonel of the officer-selection board. He barked at me, "Any good at boxing?" I answered, truthfully (at least in regard to my last appearance in the ring, in camp in America at the age of ten), "Why, yes, sir." And then he snapped, "Ever caned at school?" This time there was no gray area. The question was meant to reveal a young man with leadership potential and guts, and the right an-swer, I realized, was a lie. "Several times," I said, looking him more directly in the eye than I had looked at Otto in the billiard room ten years before.

‖ 10 ‖

I WASN'T UNACQUAINTED WITH SERVANTS. MY FATHER'S PAR-
ents had a live-in maid, called May, and in the flat over
the bank at Portchester a woman called Ellen came to
clean several mornings a week. But we were in the closing
years of the servant-employing era, as far as the English
middle class was concerned; the staff in the Spaeth household represented to me a novel order of things. Particularly impressive was the governess—the first I'd ever encountered—whose name was Fräulein von Doderer. Her
main concern was Mimi, but her duties also involved
making sure that Tony Spaeth and I got bathed and into
bed at night, and up for breakfast and off to school in
the morning. For a short while she attempted to teach
me the piano, but I was exceptionally dense and inac-
cessible when sitting next to her on the piano bench. It
may have been simply the title "Fräulein," by which we
called her, that generated in me a lack of response to
scales and chords, or to the distinction between quarter
and sixteenth notes. Or did I imagine that she was the
spearhead of the German advance into the Middle West,
and would be standing in the front garden, cheering the
panzer divisions as their tanks trundled up Runnymede
Drive? One day she got up from the bench in front of
the Steinway and stormed out of the living room, leaving behind the discordant echo of notes my leaden fingers
had just clashed out of the beautiful instrument, and
letting fly—was it in the real air or merely in my head?—
the resounding Teutonic declaration, "You are a little

English swine!" Perhaps, I later thought, there had been a larger row of which I knew nothing, but suddenly featured as the last straw. Eloise had hired Fräulein von Doderer because she came from "a very superior Austrian musical family." This was a recommendation that may have seemed fine in the abstract but proved prickly in the flesh. Otto enjoyed sitting with Von Doderer, as Eloise called her, talking in German about composers, conductors and orchestras, often at times when she should have been attending to her job. She braided her long blond-brown hair and coiled it over her head, so that she looked like the heroine of a Wagner opera. Then she started coming down to breakfast in her negligee and insisted that Artie make her bed for her. It seemed to Eloise that the governess was beginning to be a houseguest, and then, to crown it all, she got whooping cough (TS and I had it, and presumably passed it on to her) and decided that she warranted absolute attention as an invalid.

That was it. Miss Sjolin replaced her—Marta Sjolin, whose hand on the punitive hairbrush was memorable, but whose skill with the spatula, serving up Swedish pancakes stuffed with loganberries, was more so. She was a fine swimmer, and it was with her that I used to run onto the long sand bar of Nauset beach during the summer of 1941, when the Spaeths rented two adjacent gray-shingled cottages facing out over Pleasant Bay, Chatham—and there, wading into deeper and deeper pools left by the tide and warmed by the sun to a temperature far more friendly than that of the sea waves that splashed in from Portugal, learned how to swim. Mimi, Miss Sjolin and I had come by train to Cape Cod, while the rest drove in the Buick. Going in or out of the house, I ran first to Miss Sjolin to say hello or goodbye. "We are Europeans," she said to me once. "We know things the Americans do not know." But she didn't tell me what these things were.

Miss Sjolin liked Cape Cod. She thought Massachusetts was similar to Sweden—or at any rate more so than Ohio, which did not appeal to her. When her brother came out from Boston to visit her, he rented a tandem bicycle and took me for a short ride on it before bearing his sister away for the day. "One day you will be big enough to take Marta for a ride," he said, which did not satisfy me. Her brother reminded her of Sweden too, and when he left she was less happy than before. Moreover, there were increasing numbers of children to look after when the Houks arrived—friends of the Spaeths from Dayton, who rented a tiny house along the beach while their children moved in with us, "for company," said Eloise. I shared a room with Johnny Houk—eight years old, like me—who impressed me one afternoon by drawing a train with sixty-two separate freight cars. Then the children of another family arrived—the Sheeds, an Anglo-American couple who ran a Catholic publishing house in New York. Underlying the population pressure was an intermittently demonstrated dispute between Miss Sjolin and her employer about bringing up Mimi. Miss Sjolin had firm Swedish prejudices—for example, she thought that taking the baby for a ride in the car could be most injurious; and Eloise was not about to knuckle under to Nordic dictates of that sort. It was announced in August that Miss Sjolin would not be going back to Dayton with us.

Meanwhile we climbed the lighthouse, swam in dog-paddle races at the beach club, had a clambake and fireworks party on the beach on July 4, and went fishing. Fish replaced planes in my head for a while: I thought about sea robins and flounder and tinker mackerel and lugworms. Tony Spaeth and I went on several fishing trips with an older boy who had the use of an outboard-powered skiff, and one afternoon in the sound behind Monomoy Island got caught in a summer storm. We sat on the floorboards holding towels and buckets over our heads as the rain came down in silver torrents, the thunder growled, and lightning now and then heightened the apprehensive expression on the face of our twelve-year-old skipper, who was presumably worried that the old Johnson might stop in the downpour or that the waves into which we were heading might swamp the boat. TS and I were put to work bailing. A can of worms upset. I bailed a heap of slithering creatures into the drink. When we got back, Miss Sjolin was too relieved to be cross; her idea of what was fitting for the occasion included hot milk and whiskey for storm-soaked small boys. And then straight to bed.

I can now see Miss Sjolin's point about Ohio—its inlandness. Chatham appealed to my own water-inclined nature—affected by the brine in the blood that is the birthright supposedly of all Englishmen. I enjoyed the pleasures of dabbling in sand and having salt dry out tart and sticky on my skin, and the damp in everything. I liked the weathered clapboard and shingled houses, the dunes of the huge beach running north to Provincetown, and even the fog that drifted up over the coarse green grass of the lawn and seemed—with the sun filtering through it—to hold the gray houses in suspension. I didn't connect the ocean I could see beyond the sand bar with the one I had crossed ten months before.

The only thing that threatened to distort that summer was fear—I was suddenly seized by a tremendous terror. Someone—Johnny Houk, perhaps, or Wilfrid Sheed—had brought some comics featuring a character called Dr. Doom. His name was printed in wavery letters, effectively designed to increase one's fright. The doctor rose from the grave at dead of night and prowled around small towns, like Chatham. He either got the dead in graveyards to come to life or induced people to descend into tombs, where he used their vital properties for his own fiendish purposes. By one of those leaps of the imagination that it is possible to make, no doubt more easily at the age of eight, primitively associating one thing with another—like bad luck with stepping on cracks in the sidewalk, or the thought that something good one wanted to happen would not come about if one thought about it (but how *not* to think about it?)—I came to believe that Dr. Doom inhabited the cellar under the house we were in.

The house was built on the hillside that sloped down to the beach. Thus the front door, facing the road, was at ground level, but the back door, facing the sea, opened onto a porch from which a flight of wooden steps led down to the lawn, past a door that went into the cellar—there, at the rear, at lower ground level. On a nail driven into the door (painted a faded tile red) hung a cork lobster-pot float and a short length of manila warp. Going down the back steps, I would whiz past that door. I tried to avoid looking at it. Nothing would convince me to go through it into the cellar. I was sure the sunken-eyed cadaverous face of the dread doctor would loom out of the cobwebbed darkness, and his white hands would reach out for me.

Finally I had to tell; Miss Sjolin asked me to put the lawn rake away down there, and I blurted out something of my fear to her. Together we went down to the cellar, and she went in first. Only some garden implements, a pair of oars, some old cans of paint, a spare tire for a car. I no longer had to run past the cellar door, and I should have felt relieved; but in a way, as when one loses something—even very painful—that possesses one entirely, I felt disappointed to have lost my fear.

‖ 11 ‖

One of our visitors that summer in chatham was my godfather, Roy Bower. Roy had moved on to Shanghai when my parents married. A massive, richly carved teak chest arrived from China as his wedding present to them, fastened with a mysterious lock that required agile wrist work as well as illustrated instructions to open it. The chest was crammed with objects Roy had found in one place or other in his Asian travels: carved seals, a bolt of silk, embroidered pictures, incense burners, each with a small card on which Roy had written notes about the object's origin. With three heavy seals, for example, made from a pink-brown stone that resembled marble, decorated with incised ideograms and carved creatures that looked like lions crossed with dragons, Roy's card read: "Hangkow—soapstone seals (used on ink pads, not with wax). This set may have belonged to a student, as the words are poems extolling the benefits of scholarship. The shopkeepers have discovered that foreigners use these seals for bookends. Therefore they now make them for this purpose, much better carved than these, but lacking the Chinese characteristics. The real seals are difficult to find. These came from a secondhand dealer's in an alley of Shanghai."

My mother's first name was Phyllis, and she had curly, even frizzy hair. Roy—whose devotion to her was manifested in what she always called "the treasure chest"—used to call her Phuzz. He was born in Spokane, Washington; studied at Montpelier University in France; became a career officer in the U.S. Foreign Service; and at every post he went to, organized theatrical productions (particularly of Shakespeare), which he directed; he never married, and readily accepted the invitation to become a godparent. Throughout my childhood, gifts periodically arrived from Roy. He was stationed in Stockholm when I was two or three and sent me a pair of stuffed fabric horses and riders, made in Lapland. While he was in Munich I received from him a Shuco toy car, black and chrome, with a clockwork motor and a steering wheel that actually turned the front wheels. Later he bought memberships for me and Bridget in a book club intended for American children, the Golden Hours Book Club, which every two months or so sent us volumes like Hendrik Van Loon's *Story of Tolerance* or *A Child's Saga of the Nations.* One such book I still have was Hope Muntz's enthralling novel about King Harold of England, *The Golden Warrior,* which took the second son of Godwin, Earl of Wessex, from his position of leader of Edward the Confessor's housecarls to his death, as King of the English, on the battlefield near Hastings. Once a year Roy wrote a long letter to me, sometimes couched in fairly grown-up language, a little ahead of my age, but also in a man-to-man tone that made me want to reach up and join in at that level. In February 1941 he ended a long letter from Munich in this way:

> I am quite well, and I think everything is going to turn out the way we wish it to. One of these days you and I will have a meeting and a grand old beano. Meanwhile, we must all keep our chins up. The best thing you can do is to enjoy every minute of your visit in the USA, and be ready to talk for hours when you get home.

Roy was one of a number of U.S. consular officials ordered to leave Germany in late June 1941—some accused of spying, some of passing on to the English and French the German war plans, and one or two, as in Roy's case, "of making disapproving observations concerning Germany in the presence of German persons." That sounded very much in character for Roy. To my mother he had already written expressing his feelings that the Germans wanted to be slaves: "They believe only in ruthless courage and grab. That won't win a war. It's only brute courage, which won't hold out when matched against a better man." He came out of Germany with one hundred and twenty-four other Americans by way of Lisbon and the ship *West Point,* glad to leave what he called "that beastly nation"—hating and loathing "not only Hitler and the Nazis, but the whole people. I hope they'll be destroyed forever."

Roy had seen what was happening to the Jews. Possibly he knew a lot more about what was going on in Germany than many Germans. He had a fury felt by a number of those who were old enough to have been acquainted with the passions and horrors of World War I, and with the hopes of the peace. He may have felt at this point in mid-'41 that his fellow countrymen were dragging their feet a little—the battle would have to be joined with the Axis powers—and he was compensating for their lethargy. When he reported to the State Department in Washington he was given a new posting, as consul in Madras, India. But with four months' accumulated leave to be enjoyed before he set off for there, he volunteered to spend some of it giving lectures, telling his compatriots (as he wrote to my parents) "a few home truths. The Eastern seaboard and the West understand that everything the U.S.A. stands for is in mortal danger from those gangsters and their slave peoples, but the Midwest still seems to fail to grasp the realities."

Roy also came to Chatham to see me. I demonstrated to

him my newly acquired swimming prowess and general well-being. Roy talked with Otto about the state of the world and found they were in agreement about many things, including the demonic spirit loose in Germany. (I have since wondered whether Roy had to adjust his antipathy to everything German, recently gained in Munich, Bavaria, in the presence of someone of Bavarian ancestry like Otto—though after visiting Chatham, Roy reported by letter to my parents of the Spaeths' great courtesy and culture, and my good fortune in being with them.) Roy also arranged to meet me in New York on my way back to Dayton in early September. Eloise drove me to Woods Hole and put me on the train, and I rode down the meandering New Haven Railroad's shoreline in care of a conductor, past bays, inlets, harbors, and small towns with white-towered churches and names such as Kingston, Stonington, Mystic and Noank—places that were (though I didn't know it then) laid down in my senses like frozen seeds of corn to germinate in a later time.

In New York, Roy and I stayed at the Hotel Earle, in Washington Square. I hadn't really seen much of the city the year before, while quartered in the Bronx, but Roy—who said that he wanted to live there one day himself—now gave me the chance. We ate in the Automat: one hardly expected the portions of food behind those little glass doors to be real when one put in a coin and lifted the door, but they just about were—or was that when, having chosen a segment of fluffy-topped lemon meringue pie, I first realized that things had several dimensions, perceptible to several senses, and in taste might not live up to the promise of appearance? We went to the summit of Radio City. Roy bought me a miniature brass model of this skyscraper and a pocket knife, inscribed "Rockefeller Center," out of which unfolded can opener, corkscrew, screwdriver and several blades. With Roy's aunt, Alice McAfee, a New Yorker, we rode down Fifth Avenue on the open top of a double-decker bus and took a ferry to Bedloe Island, where we climbed to the tiara of the Statue of Liberty and looked out at the shipping-filled harbor. I admired the De Soto cabs with sunshine roofs through which one looked up at the huge overhanging cornices and the fire escapes, zigzagging down the fronts of buildings, while the streets, in which the yellow cabs jostled with one another, were pocketed with potholes and with orifices from which steam rose. Roy and I sent a telegram to my parents, celebrating our excursion. And Roy shortly thereafter turned up in Dayton, on his Midwest speaking tour, to give a lecture at Wright Field. Otto showed him around Dayton Tool and Engineering, and photographs were taken of Roy—square-faced, bespectacled —looking diplomatically interested as Otto explained the working of a Pratt & Whitney jig-boring machine, with TS and me looking on, really fascinated.

I feel I must follow Roy's life, as I perceived it in small glimpses, into a later period. I received a letter from him at Christmas 1946, from Madras, where he was still in charge of the consulate. He was replying to a letter of mine in which I had included some drawings. Roy admired several but criticized one as plodding and fussy. He wrote:

> The trick is to say one's piece in confident lines and then to say to hell with it if it's not quite what one meant to say. Don't pick at it. And the trick of tricks is the initial selection.

He was a forthright lecturer, not afraid of expressing his point of view. However, he apologized for not sending a present.

As far as I know I never had a godfather, but I certainly would have thought very poorly of him if he couldn't at least send me a Christmas card. What else are the silly chaps for? In mid-Victorian novels they used to die and leave their godchildren vast fortunes, or maybe cut them out of their wills because the kids bumped into their gouty foot. It's not a bit of use you waiting for me to leave you something in my will, for I intend to go on living for a dickens of a long time, and when I go there won't be a penny for anybody.

Poor Roy—poor oddfather, as he sometimes called himself. He had to retire prematurely from the Foreign Service a bare two years after this, because of ill health. He moved into a semibasement apartment at 299 Riverside Drive in New York. He had things wrong with his liver and his heart. (I went and looked at this building twenty-five years later, and was glad to see that his apartment wasn't below ground. The side street sloped downhill, the way the lawn had done at Chatham, and thus the front windows of Roy's apartment were at ground level on Riverside Drive.) Fortunately Roy's 1941 hope that the whole German people would be destroyed had not come to pass, for it was a German doctor—a prewar refugee from Germany whom Roy had met in India—who moved in and looked after Roy in exchange for lodging while he studied for his New York State medical exams. And though the figure of death, like Dr. Doom, was now stalking Roy, there was no fear or self-pity in his letters. His sight went but he wrote to say that he was pleased with some photographs I had sent to him:

> I can picture you clearly, so don't hesitate to send me photos from time to time because I'll never be able to see them with my own eyes. It's a delightful surprise to find that I "see" quite well indeed with other folks's peepers.

Had anyone said that to me before I lost my sight, I'd have felt a stab of pity and thought how brave they were. It just ain't that way at all!

Roy went on (in what was only here and there a mistyped letter) to note that this proved to him once again that accepted ideas often didn't correspond with actual facts. It was smart to keep an open mind. He concluded by expressing delight in regard to a trip I was hoping to make to Paris, and suggested that I go and look at his favorite museum, the Carnavalet municipal museum. His pet item there was "a newspaper which in one column almost casually mentions that Marie Antoinette was being guillotined that day and in another column prints an advertisement of pigs for sale, just as though nothing unusual was happening in the French capital."

The last correspondence I had that had to do with Roy came from Spence, Hotchkiss, Parker & Duryee, a firm of Wall Street lawyers. Despite his intention of living a long life, he died early in 1950. Despite his threats to leave no money, he left a small sum, which included bequests to his two godchildren—my sister Bridget and me. I used Roy's $250 to buy a steamship ticket to New York in 1955, when I graduated from the university and returned to America to seek my fortune. The last lesson he got across to me was that—to misquote his favorite playwright—the good that men do may well live after them.

|| 12 ||

AT THE TIME MANY PEOPLE WERE CONCERNED ABOUT THE
effect on children of "evacuation"—that unlikably named
wartime condition. Loneliness, deracination, displacement
and various forms of trauma were discussed. Psychologists
prepared to deal with bed-wetting, temper tantrums and
other types of attention-getting, such as stealing and self-
inflicted injuries. Perhaps some children did suffer in
these ways as a result of being uprooted and set down in
strange places, but many of those I've run into since—at
least those fortunate enough to have been shipped to
America—talk rather of what an interesting time they had.
We were immensely adaptable. Perhaps the most serious
problem was that when the day came, some did not want
to go home.

That did not include me, but neither do I recall spending a great deal of time in Dayton wondering about the
life in England that I was missing. At night I prayed for
my parents and sister in a "Dear God" roundup that included Otto and Eloise Spaeth, my Aunt Connie, my
grandparents, the Spaeth girls—Marna, Debbie and Mimi
—and the governess of the moment (Miss Sjolin's replace-
ment was Mademoiselle Roger, a sweet Frenchwoman who
patiently played countless games of Chinese checkers with
TS and me, and who did not practice corporal punishment). I also asked God to bless Tony Spaeth and of
course myself, and suggested that He do His best to bring
the war to an end, somehow without associating that
event with the thought that peace would enable me to

return to Bailey life in Park Gate, Hampshire. In the Spaeth household there was always a lot going on. The pleasures and concerns of every moment preoccupied me and prevented me from brooding on my missing English life. Or do I forget? Have I wiped clean from my memory those times when I lay awake wondering about my mother and sister in the air-raid shelter or standing in line for groceries, and thinking about my father who had at last managed to get taken into the army? I trusted in their safety. *Nothing* would happen to them.

Tony Spaeth and I walked four blocks to school in the morning, ran home to 630 Runnymede for lunch at eleven-forty, ran back to school, and then dashed home again a little after three. Harman Avenue Grade School (Gretchen Smalley, Principal) was the establishment we went to that first year—a two-story brick edifice forming a three-sided courtyard, with a columned portico across the opening, and attended by two hundred and fifty-six students. For a few days I was tried out in the second grade, more or less my age level, but then put into the third grade, whose teacher was Miss Charlotte Seitner, where I was the youngest. Miss Seitner and I got on well, even when she was scolding me for having an untidy desk. That winter, when I was in bed with whooping cough for two weeks, Miss Seitner figured in the daydreams or semi-delirium in which I traveled off between whoops to mina-reted Eastern palaces with fountains splashing in arcaded courtyards, with veiled women, and men with scimitars guarding the chamber where Miss S. was being held against her will and I was about to rescue her—the effects perhaps of seeing such movies as *Sinbad the Sailor* or early exposure to the myth of St. George, dragon and beautiful princess.

Our class project that year was Indians. We made wampum with beads and string, drew teepees, wigwams, pueblos and long houses. Miss Seitner directed us in a play called *How an Indian Chief Is Chosen,* and took a photograph (which I sent home) showing me and my boy classmates doing various heel-and-toe exercises in the guise of being Indian braves performing a dance, while Marilyn Sargent, Jane Rich, Fredricka (Dricka) Haswell and the other girls looked on. When I reached the sixth grade at Harman School, after two in-between years at a Catholic school on the other side of town, our class project was maps. (I had missed dinosaurs in fourth grade and volcanoes in fifth.) Mr. E. Bennett Owen, our teacher, covered all of one long wall of the classroom with brown paper and set us to work making a map of the world, Mercator projection. We were each allotted a section, squared off so that we could scale up outlines from an atlas. My part of the world was in the Far East. I drew islands—the Celebes, the Moluccas, the Philippines, the Indonesian archipelago. "Archipelago," I said aloud to myself, causing Harry Ebeling, who was standing next to me working on Burma, to look at me as I at first laughed at the word and then became thoughtful at the complicated and mysterious sound of it.

Otto and Eloise no doubt had in mind our religious education and our immortal souls when they sent us to Notre Dame (pronounced *no*-ter dayme) Country Day School, run by nuns. But the ride in a high yellow bus there and back took us away from our Oakwood pals and it was short on masculine activities, which is why we went back to Harman Avenue after two years with the Sisters. My high moment at Notre Dame was when I was picked for the team to compete in the Ohio school spelling championships. We were taken to Columbus, the state capital. I reached the finals in my age group and was beginning to wonder how I would handle the glory of victory, when I was asked to step into the limelight again. Crowded hall,.

expectant faces. The man putting the words to me asked if I would spell the word "bin"—or at least that was what the word sounded like. "I beg your pardon," I said, not absolutely sure of his pronunciation. "Bin," he said. "Oh," I said—that was simple enough. "B-I-N." "No," he said. "B-E-E-N. Bin." I got a few more right and then another American punch was delivered. Spell "neighbor." I unthinkingly followed British practice and put a *u* in the last syllable. Out I went. British Ace Shot Down. No happy landings.

There were other American rituals to come to terms with. We had acquired political campaign buttons on first arriving, and, fancy-free, wore them for Willkie and Roosevelt in our gray-suit lapels. At school, the Pledge of Allegiance took place first thing in the morning—we raised our right hands, in a sort of Indian salute, while the Stars and Stripes, the Star-Spangled Banner, hung in listless folds from its gilt-tipped pole in one corner of the room, and we recited the catechism of faith about one nation indivisible, and Fred Young, catching my abstracted eye, grinned at me and I tried to keep a straight face. Flag worship was new to me. On the other hand, the words to "America" were sung to the same tune as the familiar "God Save the King." And some of what I learned then was in many senses memorable. Just as in later years at school in England—though in principle excused as a Catholic from morning prayers—I took into my heart the words of Protestant hymns like John Bunyan's "He Who Would Valiant Be" and was eager to take my turn reading the lesson from the King James Bible, so at Harman School I found myself in sympathy with the rebel side in the American Revolution and enjoyed the great documents and orations of American history. Consequently, several epochs of my life later, snatches of the Declaration of Independence or the Gettysburg Address come back to me while shaving in my

London bathroom, or walking along a French street: ". . . the pursuit of happiness . . ."; ". . . our fathers brought forth on this continent . . ."

Photographs form a substitute memory. Our past has been expanded by them. Possibly it is sometimes the photograph itself we remember (tricycling along the promenade at Torquay at the age of three) rather than the incident that was being photographed. But a photograph may also trigger an act of remembrance. The faces that stare out of faded sepia-toned photographs a century old are like the peat-preserved bodies that have been drawn from the bogs of Denmark, relics of real life, real death. The photos prompt a compassion that surges around the people preserved there on film. "So that was me," I think now, with a stab of sorrow for the child in a feathered war bonnet who felt then no pity for himself but was having a fine time showing off before Marilyn, Jane and Dricka. The girls, I remember, had an Indian corn-harvest ceremony of their own, which was performed next.

|| 13 ||

DRICKA HASWELL AT ONE POINT HAD BRACES—THOSE WIDE, railroad-track type bands that were meant to pull back the front teeth and correct the effects of heredity or thumb-sucking. She had straight brown hair. While deep in a spring-afternoon sixth-grade trance, lettering the word "Celebes," I was conscious of Dricka farther along the wall, in another part of the world. I was just eleven. A few months before, the first stirrings of interest in girls as different beings had drawn me to the telephone in the room where Otto sometimes developed and printed his own photographs, in order to dial Marilyn Sargent's telephone number. I warmed up the requisite courage by first calling the Oakwood Drugstore and asking the proprietor if he had Prince Albert in the can. The proprietor clearly recognized my voice as that of one too young to be interested in smoking a pipe tobacco, canned or otherwise packaged, but sportingly said he had and was already hanging up (since he was a veteran of such pranks) when I brought forth the punchline, "Well, let him out, then." Marilyn answered the phone. Perhaps the time was just starting for her when life would revolve around the phone ringing and then talking on it for hours. I imagine we discussed matters of such consequence as whether she was bringing peanut-butter and marshmallow sandwiches on the school trip to the Art Institute, and what Mr. Owen, our teacher, had said to Harry Ebeling and Orval Cook for fighting in the corridor. I felt a funny sort of glow, as

I hung up, that was unlike the feeling I had when talking to any other of my friends.

This feeling was in no conscious way connected with what we knew about sex. Girls in our minds were not related to women—though we saw, for instance, Mimi in the bath, and knew that the feminine anatomy was unlike our own. Tony S. and I had learned from Debbie something about the way the human race ensured its survival. The news was passed on to us one afternoon in the front garden, behind the low hedge that ran next to the sidewalk, where Debbie found us working on our soapbox racing cars (these we drove, impelled by gravity, down the bumpy footpath of Runnymede hill). Clearly bursting with information that she herself must have recently come by, she told us the facts of life then and there. The ins and outs of the matter were fascinating, and worth being amazed about for a few minutes, anyway, before TS and I went back to the serious business of putting a wheel on its axle, and trying to get the axle to remain fastened to the wooden chassis with hammered-over nails. We stored the information away, and felt no suspicion of how soon we were to be consumed by aspirations, anxieties, commitments and delights that all followed on from there.

Certainly neither the funny feelings nor the newly acquired facts had much to do, at that stage, with activities like dancing classes at the Botts Dancing School in an old, mansard-roofed house downtown. There, dressed up in jacket and tie, the boys were lined up on one side of the big room and the girls in frilly dresses along the other. "Now, *walk* over and ask a young lady for a dance in the correct manner," Miss Bertha Botts commanded. *"No need to run,* Bill Bettcher!" Although we were supposed to approach the girls directly opposite us, there was a tendency to try to reach the prettier or perhaps simply the lighter, more nimble ones first. Miss Botts's voice abbreviated the moments of decision: "Now a fox trot." And thus we acquired the foundations of social grace, the rudiments of expertise in the rhumba and waltz, and experience of the expressions on girls' faces when we stepped on their toes. The sweat of our ten- or eleven-year-old palms ran together.

Each Easter Sunday Eloise organized an Easter-egg hunt. It was an occasion we looked forward to all the more because we had given up candy for Lent. It was something to think about during the long, long Mass of the Transfiguration on Good Friday; we could anticipate, in a day and a half's time, the end of deprivation and on Monday at least the return of Baby Ruths and Tootsie Rolls. Meantime there would be the hunt for chocolate eggs hidden by the Easter bunny, that scarcely credible figure of spring, in the scrappy green grass and paltry hedges of the front yard. We were each given a small wicker basket. TS and I were given the additional instructions not to be too pushy with invited children, and this sat disagreeably with our basic determination to find more eggs than anyone else and so win an additional prize. I had an extra difficulty. Was I to let Dricka Haswell find the egg, close to her left toe, that I had already spotted? I solved that acute moral and romantic dilemma by picking up the egg, wrapped in shiny metallic-blue tinfoil, and putting it in my basket. An admiring glance later on from Dricka for the winner, assuming it was I, would be worth more than a quick and quickly forgotten thanks in the heat of the action now.

Otto and Eloise must have perceived early signs of adolescence coming on in me: legs were suddenly too long for short "pants," as Americans called them. TS and I were rigged out in long pants together. And one evening when I was in the bath Otto came in and delivered a speech of mysterious portent about clean thoughts and respect for the body and not letting oneself be carried away by sudden urges. I wasn't sure what an unclean thought was, and the presence of a large cake of Ivory soap (advertised as "Ninety-nine and forty-four one hundredths per cent pure") floating in the tub didn't help clarify matters, since the cleanliness it betokened was purely physical—or could it also permeate the mind? Ceremonies of incipient manhood. I didn't tell Tony Spaeth about this visit from his father—TS wasn't as old as I was. (And perhaps TS didn't tell me.)

‖ 14 ‖

OTTO WAS AN INTENSELY GOD-FEARING MAN. HE GOT ACROSS to us his respect for the Almighty and his skepticism for some of those who were His ministers on earth. Otto was at once a progressive Catholic layman and a conservative Catholic believer; where the church made contact with society he was prepared to fight it hard, if need be, but where it told him what to believe he abandoned himself to faith. Later he was to battle the Catholic Legion of Decency in regard to film censorship. Yet if the Pope issued an edict on a matter of doctrine, Otto would fall into line. He would talk about it, thrash about with it, but eventually convince himself of its truth—or of his duty to accept it as truth. During the war he often said that the Pope should be asked to play a part in the final peace settlement. "The word 'God' did not appear in the documents of the Versailles treaties," Otto declared. "Maybe we can expect a bit more if this peace is written by men who acknowledge His existence."

At mass Otto would kneel at the aisle end of the pew, with one elbow resting on the top of the pew and his hand cupped under his chin, the fingers covering his cheek, eyes either closed or staring at the altar above the priest's head, as if he were one of those donor figures in a medieval triptych, representing, say, the laity in the presence of a saint. Just before the offertory Otto would bring out of his trousers pocket a neatly folded silver-clipped stack of bills, from which he would peel one as the collection plate came by and with the casual gesture of a card-player raising the stakes drop it—generally a five- or ten-dollar bill—on the mound of coins and white envelopes with their unknown contributions. After the service he and Eloise (whose Catholicism was also family-rooted; her maiden name was O'Mara) would talk about the sermon, quite often in tones of weariness or exasperation; but this critical attitude toward the intelligence of the parish priest didn't affect their diligence in attending mass or in making sure that their children, including me, performed their religious duties.

My mother (*née* Molony), on marrying a non-Catholic (a negative term which fairly accurately described my father's religious status; he was baptized in the Church of England but was genially agnostic), promised to ensure the Catholic upbringing of any children the marriage produced. My father didn't mind. The first proper school I went to after kindergarten was St. Benedict's, in Fareham, run by nuns, and if it hadn't been for the war I would have gone on from there to St. John's College, a school in Portsmouth where most of the teachers were monks. My mother, I and Bridget, as she got older, used to attend mass in Fareham in a sooty stone church in a street behind the bus station. When we got home my father sometimes greeted us with wisecracks about Father So-and-so and the communion wine, and what the Pope or the bishop had told us to do this week—remarks that my mother accepted good-humoredly. In Dayton, as I said earlier, my religion was a reason why I was acceptable to the Spaeths as a foster child, and the Spaeths, on the same grounds, were judged suitable as foster parents by the local Catholic welfare organization, to which had been delegated by the U.S. Committee for the Care of European Children the responsibility for keeping an eye on me. At Notre Dame Country Day School, religious instruction was part of the package, and Tony S and I were taught how to serve at mass as altar boys, instructed how to ring the bells at the right moment and bring the cruets of wine and water to the priest when needed. After returning to Harman School we had special once-a-week lessons from a monk at a downtown Catholic high school to keep us on the theological straight-and-narrow.

Like many of the things that are forced on children, religious activities seemed to me mostly boring and banal, manifestations of the inscrutable power of adults rather than of the omnipotence of the Almighty. But there were moments when I felt swept away, either on a cloud of unreasoning tranquillity or to the edge of a cliff from which I could look over into the abyss. I could sit in church, listening to the sonorous Latin phrases—*Introibo ad altare Dei* and similar incantations—while pleasantly daydreaming, my eyes continuing to scan the interestingly printed missal with its silk page markers, its red-ink and black-ink sections, keeping just conscious of the moments at which I was supposed to sit or stand or kneel or make the sign of the cross. That was one side of it. On the other, darker side there were Sundays when mass had a different effect. Then the missal was something one lost one's way in. The church suddenly felt too small. The air was thick and heavy, laden with incense, sweet, and damp with heat. The bells jangled nervously. The windows—why were they barely open? How I would have liked to prize them apart. Meanwhile my ears were filled with the rattling voice of the priest running the words together in a vehement jumble. One Sunday morning in the church at Chatham these things came together in an oppressive rush. My throat was dry. There was abruptly no room, no space around me. I felt hot, cold. The air clouded as all my senses went muzzy and then blank. I tumbled over.

When I came to, I was sitting on the grass at the edge of the church parking lot, the red Buick somewhere behind me shining with the total strength of the noon sun. For a few hours I was treated gently, tentatively, as one might treat someone who is different. Was this a form of religious experience or simply another example of my failure to cope with certain enclosed situations, as on long car journeys? (I had thrown up in the back of the Cadillac when driving to Decatur. For this reason I had been asked to join the train party to Cape Cod.) Perhaps, I decided, it was to do with being "highly strung"—I had overheard Miss Seitner and Eloise talking about me one day, and for a while had a vision of myself as some sort of musical prodigy, despite Fräulein von Doderer's contrary testimony. Perhaps (I thought later) it was the Protestant half of me making itself felt. Perhaps (I thought later still) it was because I had fasted for communion and had not yet had my daily quota of Wheaties.

Brother Bernard of Chaminade High School went through the catechism with me during my sixth-grade year. At these sessions I became aware of a layer of unease beneath the assurance with which the good brother dealt out sections of Christian doctrine, to be memorized for the following week. It was as if he detected the beginnings of doubt in some of my difficulties in remembering words that for me had no breath of reality in them. In fact, I found it difficult to frame questions that adequately fitted the bafflement resulting from the collision of my burgeoning reason and the rigmarole we were going through. Brother Bernard's attempts to sort out puzzles that existed for me—as, for example, how one could be granted, in return for making a sign of the cross, an "indulgence" of one hundred days off one's stay in Purgatory (or, with the addition of holy water, three hundred days), when Eternity, in which Purgatory existed, was essentially a timeless state—generally consisted in repeating the relevant paragraph and associated sections leading up to it.

" 'What do we mean when we say in the Apostles' Creed that Christ descended into hell?' " read out Brother Bernard, in his role as the successor to St. Thomas Aquinas and numerous church authorities who had wrestled with these knotty problems.

" 'When we say that Christ descended into hell,' " I said, with a bit of help from the right page of the catechism, " 'we mean that, after He died, the soul of Christ descended into a place or state of rest, called Limbo, where the souls of the just were waiting for Him.' But what had they been doing there all that time, Brother?"

"Ah, Tony, what is the next question in the catechism?"

"It says, 'Why did Christ go to Limbo?' "

"And the answer?"

" 'Christ went to Limbo to announce to the souls waiting there the joyful news that He had re-opened Heaven to mankind.' "

"Good," said Brother Bernard, as if this settled everything.

Clearly a drama was involved, with dramatic characters, and a universe with interesting levels, such as Heaven and Hell. We had for fellow, God-made creatures the angels, "created spirits, without bodies, having understanding and free-will," as the guidebook told me. One of these spirits apparently kept an eye on me, protected me from harm, and inspired me to do good and possibly to bedevil Brother Bernard with another question—"How do we know they have free will?"—which made him bring forth, with a wry smile, his ultimate answer: "That is a supernatural mystery."

"But—"

"And, Tony, as you no doubt remember, 'A supernatural mystery is a truth which we cannot fully understand, but which we firmly believe because we have God's word for it.' "

Later, when shame and doubt superseded this innocent bravado, it was embarrassment that often swept over me in church, especially if I was up on stage as one of the servers, sitting where I could feel the eyes of the congregation shift on to me as Father Frawley in Fareham rolled his broguish tongue around words like "carnal knowledge" or "the Virgin's womb." Even the word "flesh," which seemed to occur a good deal in both Testaments, brought on a blush—a deep red suffusing my skin from neck to scalp—that was perceptible, I felt sure, to the entire congregation as they viewed me against the familiar altarscape. I would have liked somewhere to hide.

I know now that one of the consolations of religion (if not of being in church) is its ability to furnish a hiding place for man, a spot where he can shelter, feeling a little protected against the crushing immensity of the stars, the weight of the galaxies, the mass of the unknown and unknowable. And I came to feel that when Catholicism offered a strangeness commensurate with the original mystery of life, it more nearly matched my own demands, such as they were—incoherent, imprecise and unappeased by such mechanisms as confession. Latin, immanent with its own mystery and history, seems to me the better language for this purpose, and I can see why the Catholic traditionalists wish to retain the Latin mass.

In the early 1950s Otto and I once or twice tacked conversationally into this area of things. I courteously tried to oppose to his faith my disbelief in the church and he tried to treat my attitude as undergraduate and temporary. He was confident that once a Catholic, always a Catholic; I would come around. Now Otto is no longer alive to talk to. Possibly he would find me a little less intractable now—not that "organized religion" holds much of a spell for me, but I like singing hymns, a comradely habit picked up in nondenominational American camps or British, mostly

Protestant, schools. I like the chance to sit and let my thoughts wander, which a church, and the sound of a parson's voice, afford. And I have reached the point, perhaps physiological as much as metaphysical, at which I feel the unknown (that was still close to me as a child) once again begin to loom around me. I am aware that I have probably passed halfway round the board; there is no second voyage around the course. It is a quick push off the edge and a presumably unconscious plummet into the gulf of the dark. *Introibo* . . . into what?

But Otto would be glad that I have come this far, and I can see his assured look, as if he were saying, "You will get there yet."

‖ 15 ‖

WITHIN DAYTON WE HAD OUR OWN TERRITORIES AND TRACKS through them, mostly in Oakwood, our leafy suburb which had its own municipal organization: city hall, police and fire departments, and school system. There were the well-known blocks through which Tony S. and I zigzagged to school; our newspaper route; and the trolley-bus line out to the Far Hills movie theater, where on Saturday mornings we watched films like *Viva Cisco Kid!,* with Cesar Romero, or *Shooting High,* with Jane Withers and Gene Autry. This was close to the shopping center where Otto, the first Howard Johnson's franchise holder in those parts, built an orange-roofed restaurant—interesting to us mostly because of the twenty-eight flavors of the ice cream; my favorite was peppermint-stick. Dayton's trams—or street-cars, as they were called—were being phased out as the war began, leaving electric trolleys and regular buses, but many of the main streets still had tram tracks, which were perilous for inattentive bike riders. For a year or so TS and I delivered the Dayton *Journal-Herald,* the afternoon sister paper of the Dayton *Daily News.* We were outfitted with burlap newspaper bag and chromed change dispenser. We took turns at picking up papers from Bob Parks, the Oakwood distributor, in the back room of his drugstore near Oakwood City Hall (just around the corner from Harman School). We quickly learned the art of rolling a paper into as tight a cylinder as its size allowed, tucking in one edge so that the paper stayed (with luck) rolled up as it was flung from the sidewalk across the front lawn onto (with more luck) the porch or doorstep. Those projectiles that went too far astray we generally retrieved and dispatched again; those that fell only slightly short stayed put. We got to know as we cycled in and out along the driveways, sidewalks and road edges the dogs that were friendly and those that were not. I have to this day an antipathy toward Alsatians, the original cause being a wolflike beast in Schantz Avenue that had apparently been trained to chase newspaper boys on big-balloon-tired Schwinn bikes with coaster brakes, gaining on them fast over several hundred yards, fangs bared, finally to sink its teeth into their thighs. I dropped that house, and street, from my route. Another confidence-sapping aspect of the job—which was advertised as training youngsters in the American virtues of self-reliance and business management—was that week in and week out I was unable to keep my accounts straight. Even when the number of customers remained stable, as it did most of the time outside vacations, the amount of money TS and I collected on Saturday afternoons fluctuated considerably. After I had paid Bob Parks out of the total ejected from the quarters, dimes and nickels compartments of my change dispenser, the amount left over as deliverer's profit was never the same. Perhaps it had something to do with tips, which people possibly gave us without mentioning it. Maybe I sometimes asked them for the wrong amount—the seven-times multiplication table was a basic need for this job, and one of my weak points. For a while I also sold subscriptions to *Collier's* magazine. The straightforward reward for that task was a set of camping equipment: water canteen, mess tin and Sterno stove, useful on our commando expeditions into Old River Park, past the Jewish cemetery and the National Cash Register summer camp, or while planning counterespionage missions from our base on Talbott Hill.

The hill was directly across the road from the Spaeth

house. At its summit were the foundations of a mansion, demolished some years before, that had been the home of the Talbott family; one Talbott would serve in the United States government as Secretary of the Air Force. Where the house had stood were lawns and hedges, maintained and clipped as if the house were still there. To one side was an empty swimming pool and deserted changing rooms. Across the private drive at the back sat a large building called the Playhouse, with indoor squash courts and a small stage that was used for local community activities. Here took place Bundles for Britain bridge benefits, blood donation drives and carol concerts. From the top of the hill there was a fine, northward view toward Dayton, over the sugar maples of the NCR camp, and westward to the river and the Deeds Carillon. This was the local landmark, a concrete bell tower given to Dayton by Colonel Deeds, chairman of NCR until April 1940, and inaugurated in December 1941. Thereafter, when the wind was in the right direction, we heard ringing over the woods the sounds of the evening concerts, "with Robert E. Kline at the console," as the weekly *Oakwood Press* told its readers, playing such melodies arranged for the bells as "There's a Long, Long Trail A-winding," "Just a-Wearyin' for You," "Ave Maria," "Song of India" and "Jesus, Lover of My Soul."

The front lawn of the old mansion was the long north slope of Talbott Hill, a semiprivate greensward flanked on one side by a hedge along Runnymede Drive and at its foot by a copse of trees. Later it would be developed for housing, but for the time being it was our estate and playground. At the summit a large slab of upended rock formed the focus of various games we played there, such as prisoner's base, kick the can or capture the flag, all of which involved hiding in the undergrowth while one of us as "it" counted to a hundred, with eyes covered, and then tried to touch the other players or touch the base (or kick the can) before they could run in, shouting "Home free!," beating "it" to it. We used one of the changing rooms by the pool as our clubhouse, plotting attacks on rival gangs and working out codes and passwords. We were on the lookout for spies. (Germans had been set ashore on Long Island, near Montauk, from a U-boat.) Toward the end of the war, part of our domain was fenced off when the Playhouse was taken over by the Monsanto Corporation, for what was afterward announced to be research on nuclear fission, and there may well have been reason for spies to be in the neighborhood of Talbott Hill.

In winter when snow had covered the hill and lay in thick drifts in the copse at the bottom, we skied and sledded, made jumps and ramps out of packed snow, loaded our sleds and toboggans with snowballs, and whizzed downhill to bombard the defenders of a snow fort, built under the trees. Sometimes the snowballs had been compressed and put aside so that they had become iceballs by the time they were thrown. The air seemed to sizzle as we sledded down and, as often as not, fell off. The snow got in our boots, past the tight elastic cuffs of our one-piece snowsuits, inside our gloves, and past the edges of our wool-lined brown leather helmets onto our ears. (Headphone-type earmuffs were sought after as being more grown-up.) Dragging our Speedster sleds uphill, we constantly slipped and fell back. When we were almost numb with cold we would stagger across the road and down into the furnace room to thaw out, red-nosed and blue-cheeked, dripping, skin prickling and stinging, painfully pulling off boots with frozen fingers and unzipping the snow-encrusted bottom six inches of each leg of our snowsuits, while watching the flames leap inside the furnace doors. Hospitable heat!

Behind 630 was a surprisingly mingy yard, considering

the size of the house. It was shaded by several big trees, and little grew there. Through a tangle of shrubbery the yard merged with the backyard of the Burke family, whose large shingled house fronted on Oakwood Avenue, the street running more or less parallel with Runnymede. My contemporary among the Burke children was Mary, who had red hair and freckles and generally lived up to her reputation as a tomboy. Mary took part in the pseudomilitary activities that Tony S. and I and our friends Bill Bettcher, Harry Ebeling and the Young cousins, Tad and Fred, conducted in a heavily wooded building site on the other side of Oakwood Avenue. A track, eventually to be a road, ran through the trees to a large concrete incinerator, which looked like an army pillbox and made it easier to get volunteers for the defending side. Sitting on top of the incinerator, with its big metal lid open, you felt like Humphrey Bogart as a tank commander. We shared the raisins that had come in some real K rations TS had got from his cousin Bernard, who was in the army.

Perhaps children are less cut off from the instincts man has from his early days as full-time hunter and warrior; falling into bands of attackers and defenders, "choosing up sides," comes naturally to them. As for me, with several years spent in the shadow of Portchester Castle's Roman walls and Norman keep, I felt an almost elemental attachment to such defensible structures. It was as if I had not only memories of afternoons playing on the grass, also a cricket pitch, inside the castle walls, but further back, in my own helping of race memory, experiences under siege behind palisades and ramparts. I felt little surprise when I discovered much later that the name Bailey was that of the outer wall of a castle or of the courtyards enclosed within it, and consequently the title Bailey had been given the man in charge of that enclosed space. And now, armed

*, passport photo, age: 7½.
nmer 1940.

Tony and his mother, Phyllis Bailey, with Bridget, his sister, in the garden at Park Gate, Hampshire, spring 1940.

er Bailey, Tony's father, 'ony, in cricket gear, at 'Gate, summer 1940.

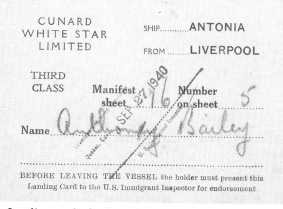

CUNARD
WHITE STAR
LIMITED

SHIP............**ANTONIA**

FROM........**LIVERPOOL**

THIRD
CLASS

Manifest
sheet........**216**

Number
on sheet........5

Name........*Anthony Bailey*

BEFORE LEAVING THE VESSEL the holder must present this Landing Card to the U.S. Immigrant Inspector for endorsement

Landing card, the Antonia. *September 1940.*

R.M.S. Antonia.

CALM AND POISED, EIGHT SMALL BRITISH REFUGEES ARRIVE HERE

Tony Spaeth, right, greets Tony Bailey in Dayton, October 1940.

Dayton's English children on the staircase at 630 Runnymede in January 1942.
From the left: Geraldine Holder, TB, Ronald Poplar, Valerie Holder, Ralph
Poplar, Maureen Cullum.

Roy Bower, the two Tonys and Otto at Dayton Tool
and Engineering, autumn 1942.

Otto in 1953.

Otto and Eloise on the bus, 1950.

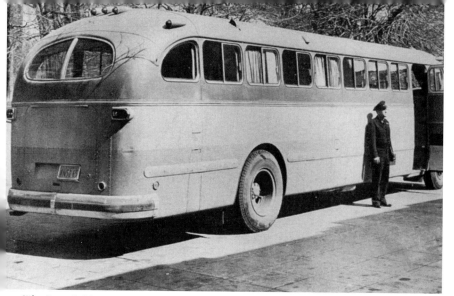

The Spaethship.

S. Truman and Otto on the 1948.

TB and Tony Spaeth on Cape Cod, 1941.

Eloise in 1937.

Tony Spaeth, Roy Bower and TB in Chatham, on Cape Cod, in August 1941.

TB, Tony Spaeth, Marna, Eloise, Mimi and Deborah in Chatham, 1941. ANDRÉ SNOW

and Mimi at Talbott Hill, Dayton, ımer 1943.

The two Tonys.

Camp Fairwood, Bellaire, Michigan, in 1943. TB in back row left; Tony Spaeth in front row right.

H.M.S. Ranee.

TB on Cape Cod in August 1941.

with a little history, I can see Mary Burke as one of those Viking women who created havoc in the early Middle Ages, laying waste the feudal settlements and terrifying the monks who wrote the contemporary chronicles—or possibly she would have done well as an Irish queen, for whose favors the local kings squabbled and went mad. Mary—when sides were chosen—was in demand. For one thing, she had a BB gun, a low-powered air rifle of the kind that Tony S. and I dearly wanted but had not yet been allowed to have. Mary could zap a root-beer bottle resting on top of the incinerator from twenty paces.

At Halloween, dressed as ghouls and goblins, we roamed the neighborhood, trick-or-treating people whether we knew them or not, our hands outstretched for candy and cookies—our trickery confined to ambushing an Oakwood black-and-white police car one year with a fusillade of eggs, and running off across Talbott Hill before the patrolmen could organize a pursuit. One October, Fred Young and I got up the nerve to ascend the steep drive to Orville Wright's house and knock on the front door under the great columned portico. No one answered, so we knocked again. Should we wait, or go? Fred and I looked at each other, our timidity increasing. But a light went on in the hall; footsteps could be heard. Then the door opened slowly and an elderly man with a gray mustache stood there. Fred and I pulled ourselves together and got out the words: "Trick or treat, Mr. Wright?"

There was a pause for reflection. How long was it since anyone had come to the recluse's house at Halloween? At last he said, "Just a minute, boys." Fred and I waited on the porch, tempted to nibble some of our candy but feeling that somehow it wasn't polite to do so when we might be on the point of getting a couple of cookies or a Hershey bar to share. Then the pioneer aviator returned

and said with a smile to the two small goblins in the doorway, "Here you are, boys." He put in Fred's hand and
mine a silver dollar apiece.

We reached the city, downtown, by trolley bus or car,
crossing through the land of the National Cash Register
Company, where small steam locomotives called stubbies
shunted freight cars from one similar factory building to
another. Downtown was a regular gridiron made interesting by narrow alleys subdividing the blocks, and certain buildings that had a surreal prominence for me
among the rest—many of them with columned fronts, like
the court house and the post office. Because of Dayton's
central geographical location and numerous printing
plants, the Dayton Post Office was given credit in many
magazines, which were registered with the Dayton post-
master as "second-class matter." We knew the whereabouts
of WHIO, the radio station that brought us the adventures
of Jack Armstrong; the two main hotels, the Van Cleve
and the Biltmore, both of which had barbershops where
we had our hair cut; and the Rike-Kummler Company, the
main department store, where we went on shopping expeditions, and once, in May 1944, to see a real P-40
fighter plane that was being exhibited on Rike's ground
floor together with a collection of captured enemy equipment. We sometimes came back home on Brown Avenue,
through the area that had a German bakery with excellent
pumpernickel, and past a ramshackle theater which advertised "Live Burlesk." Across the river from the downtown section stood the Art Institute, "two-thirds art, one-
third zoo," as Eloise described it—where we were generally
more interested in the bird and monkey cages that stood
among Twelfth Dynasty pieces. The river itself, the Miami,
curving through Dayton, was constrained by levees, concrete embankments and, farther out in the country, a series

of dams, built as a result of the great floods that devastated southwestern Ohio in 1913.

As for the neighboring countryside, with such quaintly named towns as Xenia and Yellow Springs, Antioch and Chillicothe, it seemed an adult preserve into which we would sometimes be taken on Sunday-afternoon drives to buy farm vegetables or look at things like covered wooden bridges. I associated "out of town," though it wasn't very far out, with Moraine Country Club. There Otto played golf and Tony Spaeth and I now and then caddied for him, rewarded by a small fee and a juicy sandwich and sundae in the club dining room. Beyond Moraine, ten miles out of town, was Eloise's private retreat: a tiny whitewashed one-room brick cottage, with a piece of pasture, a wooded glen and a stream running through a gully; here, we gathered, she meditated and read poetry. Hollyhocks grew around the cottage, and an artist had painted hollyhocks on either side of the door—they looked like decorations on peasant pottery cups. TS and I liked running through the field and paddling in the creek, looking for minnows and tadpoles. But we didn't go there often—it was Eloise's place.

‖ 16 ‖

LONG AFTERWARD I TOLD ELOISE THAT WHAT I REMEMBERED particularly about Otto and her in Dayton was their assurance. To me, between seven and eleven, they seemed so certain in their way of handling the world, so positive in their approach to life. It wasn't possible to imagine them being wrong. Eloise smiled at this recollection. "Well," she said, in her most forthright manner, "we often were."

When Tony Spaeth and I were taken on a walk by Eloise, we were stretched. She saw no point in walking unless you kept up a cracking pace. She was in pursuit of an ideal, and it meant not dawdling. (She wore walking shoes.) Moreover, manners were the foundation of discipline, as far as she was concerned—and possibly there was less reason for admonishing small boys who stood when adults came into the room; who held ladies' chairs for them when they sat down to dinner; who called older men "sir" (as for a while we were ordered to call Otto, as if training us for the way we should address the rest of senior mankind); who used people's names when referring to them, instead of saying "he" or "she"; and who bowed as they shook hands, saying "How do you do" clearly, not mumbling it. It was a code of conduct, early imprinted. And though this may make Eloise sound severe (and we wouldn't have dared question her authority), she was also a figure of great glamour; perhaps some of her authority resided in that.

I would knock on the door and go into her bedroom each morning to say goodbye before I went to school. Hanging over the elegant headboard of her bed would be the black silk eyeshade she wore so as not to be awakened by early-morning light. She would have on a long robe of soft, velvety stuff. On the wall, over the fireplace, was a painting of a woman seen from behind, seated in an armchair and showing her nude back, arms and shoulders. Her hair was piled up on top of her head, drawing one's gaze to the long nape of her neck. Hair and head from the rear looked like Eloise's, and Otto had bought the picture (which was by Eugene Speicher) for that reason. I would look at this picture as I chatted with Eloise, buttoned my jacket or finished tying my shoes, told her what I'd had for breakfast and promised that, yes, I would remember to write to my parents that afternoon after school and before I went out to play. In one corner of the room was a prie-dieu, with an embroidered arm rest and knee rest, at which Eloise presumably knelt to pray before she went to bed at night. As in Otto's room, there were two doors apart from the one I had come in by: one led to the dressing room, with its two rows of mirror-fronted closets facing each other, and thence to the bathroom, with a sliding glass door over the bathtub to keep shower water in; the other door led to the upper porch, over the living room.

Eloise was (and still is) an organizer. Having organized the household and arrangements for the children (Marna was at school in Cincinnati and Debbie in Tucson, Arizona), she had time for good works. (She told me later, "My mother said that if I never learned to cook, I'd never have to.") She organized the reception of me and my fellow evacuees. She organized entertainment for wounded servicemen recuperating in Dayton hospitals, and read books to blinded airmen—my mother had sent her Alice Duer Miller's verse story *The White Cliffs*, which proved useful in this way. (It told of a Rhode Island girl who marries a young English landowner. He is killed in World

War I, leaving his wife and son—who grows up to go off and fight in World War II. At one point the heroine tries to return to her New England roots but feels bound to come back to England.) Eloise organized shows of modern and religious art at the Dayton Art Institute, where she was in charge of the contemporary gallery, and she arranged an exhibition of servicemen's paintings at Wright-Patterson Field. She carried on an extensive correspondence with museums and galleries, and with artists like Walt Kuhn, who sent her drawings with notes written on them. On the phone, she had a determined way; she would answer with a terse "Yes?" and then, if the caller announced himself or herself as someone she knew, she would say more warmly, "*Oh,* yes." Later she told me that she had found Dayton dull and confining, and had reached the end of whatever she felt she could do there by the time Otto and she decided to move to New York in 1948. In New York she involved herself more deeply in the art world, writing a guidebook to American museums, becoming a trustee of the American Federation of Arts and a vice-president of the Friends of the Whitney Museum, leading foreign tours to benefit the funds of the Archives of American Art, and organizing shows at the Guild Hall in East Hampton, Long Island, where she has a summer home. She sends postcards from Easter Island or from the far reaches of China, or from Marrakech, where she is photographed relaxing in the elegant salon of a grand collector. But I think of Eloise as unrelaxed—energetic and confident, rather, as she appeared in a photo in the Dayton *Journal-Herald* in September 1940, sitting at a desk and looking like Myrna Loy, with a map of the British Isles on the wall behind her. The caption under the photo said: "What you can do for Great Britain in its hour of Greatest Need."

‖ 17 ‖

ARRIVING AT THE SPAETHS' IN LATER YEARS, HOLDING MY
suitcase in one hand and raincoat in the other, I would
stand a good chance of being met by Otto, with hammer,
picture wire and eye screws all ready, and the painting he
was intending to hang (as soon as I got there to help him)
resting against the wall. In Dayton, Tony Spaeth and I
usually held up a picture together, one of us on each side
of the Gauguin "Still Life with Profile" or the Braque
"Nature Morte." Certainly the big "Green Apples" by
Walt Kuhn, which Eloise still owns (the Gauguin and
Braque are gone), would have needed the pair of us to
lift it up while Otto stood back and decided whether it
should be higher or lower, a little to the left or right,
taking into account the position of other pictures, the placing of furniture, the effect of table lights. Being asked to
help hang a painting after suitcase was lowered and raincoat was dropped over the back of a chair was a way of
immediately being made a part of the Spaeth life again.
I felt I had resumed things where I had left; that perhaps
I hadn't left at all. Otto, leaning over the top of the
frame as we held it up, would make a little mark on the
wall. When we removed the picture he measured the distance from the wire, stretched upward, to the top of the
frame. This distance was measured again on the wall below the mark he had made, and at this new point Otto
stuck some Scotch tape on the plaster. Through this he
hammered the nail of the picture hook. The final touch
—before his enthusiasm for his double-ended thumbtacks

waned and the supply ran out—would be to press two of these into the lower back corners of the frame and then, with a spirit level ensuring that the picture was absolutely horizontal, press the bottom of it against the wall.

In Dayton all the paintings seemed to me just one part of the new world of 630 Runnymede—like the three cars and the servants. I didn't realize for some time how much the paintings meant to Otto and Eloise: that paintings and sculpture were their way of extending themselves out of the constraints of Oakwood society or Dayton industry into a more creative and cosmopolitan world. They had started collecting early on in their married life; they had begun with drawings and gone on to bigger things. During one of their prewar trips to Europe on the *Bremen* or the *Berengaria,* Otto won a great deal of money on the ship's pool, the lottery held on estimates of the ship's daily run. (This was something he won three times in six voyages.) His winnings on the first occasion enabled him to pay for their first-class passage and have money left over for pictures they saw in Paris galleries. On this and later occasions they bought with shared pleasure and soon there was a Spaeth collection, from which museums wanted to borrow; it included a Corot, a Courbet, two Gauguins, a Pissarro and a Picasso, a Cézanne and a Mary Cassatt. Eventually the Cézanne was sold to pay for a new house they had built just behind the dunes in East Hampton. The Gauguin was sold when Pabst one year failed to pay a dividend. Jack Taylor, one of Otto's best friends in Dayton, later said admiringly, "Otto's investment income went from two hundred and fifty thousand dollars a year to nothing overnight and it didn't change his life one jot. He simply sold a painting and carried on as before." However, Eloise recalls that the sale was not that painless. Throughout the night before the Gauguin was shipped off for sale, they left on the picture light over the painting, and Otto twice went down in the night to look at it.

Hanging over the mantelpiece in the living room at Dayton was a large modern-dress crucifixion scene by the British artist Mark Symons, called "Were You There When They Crucified Him?"; its predominant colors were brown and red, and the Roman centurions were in the uniform of British soldiers circa 1930. The painting gave the impression that everything happening in it was contemporary and inevitable: Christ needed to be crucified; He needed the people on hand to behave the way they did. Equally somber and memorable was a painting by Edward Hopper called "Dawn in Pennsylvania." The dark-green passenger coaches waiting at the platform seemed to have just got there, in the early morning; it was a city where one was a stranger and few were awake. There were also paintings by Beckmann and Chagall, Rouault and Léger; Matisse's cheerful "Cirque" series and a burst of flowers by Nicolas de Staël. American artists came to form an increasing part of the collection—not only Walt Kuhn and Hopper, but Charles Sheeler, Max Weber, John Marin, Karl Knaths, Reginald Marsh, Abraham Rattner, Jack Levine, Marsden Hartley, Georgia O'Keeffe, Lyonel Feininger, among others. As time went on, Otto and Eloise moved away from the big names and established reputations (although some of the names hadn't been so big when Otto and Eloise first bought them, and they stayed loyal to artists like Kuhn and Sheeler, Alexander Calder and Alexander Brook, whom they had bought early on and befriended). They bought the work of young artists, for whom it must have been a thrill not only to have sold a picture but to have learned that one of their own works was now in a collection that included Picasso and Cézanne. Otto made a point of spending two thirds of the sales price of a picture on new acquisitions; he rarely sold at a loss. Artists came to draw portraits of us children. Eloise had her portrait painted in a red evening dress, by James Chapin, and Jacques Lipchitz sculpted a fine head of Otto. Otto and Eloise visited artists in their studios, not so much to by-pass galleries (they were well acquainted with several reputable New York dealers) or to see work hot off the easel as to get closer to the artist's method of work and way of life. They were truly interested in the act of artistic creation and the individual who was capable of it. They had good eyes. They were patrons.

One of Otto's ambitions was to involve churches and businesses with contemporary art. He was a staunch supporter of the Liturgical Arts Society, which promoted the greater use of genuine art, rather than pseudoreligious artifacts, in ecclesiastical institutions. In 1950 he went to Italy, had an audience with the Pope, and in Venice looked into the possibilty of establishing there a School of Liturgical Art. Otto persuaded churches and monasteries to commission artists to make original sculpture, paintings, tapestry and stained glass, and did his best to dissuade them from ordering pastel-colored plaster statuettes from religious supply stores. He set up a foundation bearing the Spaeth name to promote these aims and to give awards for excellent religious art. He felt, too, that art should be where people came in contact with it much of the time, at their place of work. He organized conferences on the subject of "Business and Art." He tried to fire fellow industrialists with the idea that art wasn't just decoration or prestige but essential. He had prints and paintings hung in the corridors and offices of Dayton Tool and Engineering, and in the plant itself all the exposed pipes were painted bright colors, as in a Léger. When he became chairman of Metamold, an aluminum founding company in the small town of Cedarburg, Wisconsin, he arranged an art exhibition to celebrate the opening of the company's new building. The tall silo-like entrance hall had a specially commissioned Calder mobile hanging in it. Paintings were hung throughout the factory, which was thrown open on weekends for anyone to look in, to view the pictures and even buy one if they cared to. Several Cedarburg residents did so. One purchaser, a local mechanic, bought a semiabstract painting called "The Death of Agamemnon," paying for it out of his weekly wages in interest-free installments. Then, because he was living in lodgings, had no room to hang it and felt it ought to be seen, he loaned it to a Milwaukee university library.

I can see Otto standing in Metamold's entrance, watching the red vanes of the Calder mobile twist gently in the rising currents of air. I see his fingers running down the long bronze back of a statue of a girl dancer by Marino Marini; tipping the little Henry Moore bronze rocking chair containing a mother and child so that they rocked back and forth; brushing the outlines of a group of linked acrobats by Mary Callery; or tracing the mild smile on the face of a fourteenth-century limestone Madonna from France. His eyes sparkled as, looking at a picture and then at me, he asked what I felt about it, and got me to tell him.

*

|| 18 ||

THE WAR—THE REASON I WAS WHERE I WAS—WENT ON. I
followed its progress in the maps that appeared on the
front pages of the newspapers, with arrows showing pin-
cer movements and wavy black lines indicating battle-
fronts. Foggy newspaper photographs conveyed in insect-
screen monochrome a less than two-dimensional summary
of wartime incidents: a bombardment; a ship sinking; a
flag being raised; prisoners marching; a leader making a
speech. All far less real than what happened daily in the
comic strips of "Joe Palooka" or "Terry and the Pirates."
And yet just as I remembered sitting in the kitchen at
Portchester with my parents, listening to the radio—the
wireless, as it was called then, despite the wires that went
to the mains, the ground and the aerial—when it was announced that the Germans had invaded Czechoslovakia
and my father declared that war, despite Mr. Chamber-
lain, was now definitely going to come, so in Dayton I was
conscious of moments in which knowledge of critical events
came through with sudden impact: the sinking of the bat-
tleships *Prince of Wales* and *Repulse* by Japanese aircraft;
the loss of Singapore; the fall of Bataan—which Americans
reacted to the way the British had to Dunkirk. Defeats
were possibly more invigorating than victories. However,
on December 7, 1941, it had been with a mixture of indig-
nation and excitement that we heard about Pearl Harbor.
In a flash everything that FDR and Otto had been saying
for the past year came true and America was forced to join
the fight, openly, alongside Great Britain. The German

attack on Russia had been greeted similarly—there was a general feeling that in the end it would help. The odds were changing.

Yet the war was a long way from me, and my patriotism could only be fitfully expressed. Not that I tried to disguise my Englishness, or to modify my English accent—even though there were rumors that members of the Bund (an association of people with German ancestry and, we believed, pro-Nazi inclinations) were kidnapping small British children, whether for ransom, murder or to turn them into zombies or werewolves, TS and I could only guess. (The nightmares or fears of children had an unsuspected accuracy, at least in relation to what one later found the Nazi were doing to millions in the concentration camps at this time.) As for my accent, the passage of weeks and Dayton worked on it together. By the time the two pairs of gray flannel shorts I had brought from England had worn out or become too small, I was beginning to talk like a regular Oakwood third grader. Within a year I was speaking in a nasal Midwestern drawl, using words like "neat" and "snappy," and phrases such as "extra fine" and "just right," which replaced the English childhood slang of "wizard" and "topping," "blooming" and "drat." Otto said he was worried about the coarsening effect of America on what he called my fine manners, and he was anxious about what my parents would think when they heard my voice again. But my Englishness, he rightly suspected, was only temporarily latent. It existed not very far below the surface that was camouflaged with American clothes—T-shirts, lumber jacket, athletic socks, and football uniform with shoulder pads—and also likings for root beer and Dentyne, the strongest-tasting chewing gum.

Once in a while my birthright was brought up for air. Any sort of critical remark about Britain would do the trick. Tony S. and I had several fights about the weight our respective countries were pulling in the struggle against the Axis powers, foreshadowing arguments that would later take place in a wider sphere about, say, Errol Flynn's part in the movie *Objective Burma*—where his role was symbolic of what the British thought to be exaggerated American claims in the recapture of that part of the Far East from the Japanese. TS and I found ourselves discordant on such issues as the right way to swing your arms when marching; he favored the snappy, American across-the-body swing, while I preferred the straight-back-and-forth, fist-raised-as-high-as-the-shoulder British method. Moreover, when talking one day of ships, perhaps just after the *Normandie* caught fire and the great debonair liner with its rakish funnels was left a burned-out hulk alongside a Manhattan pier, I mentioned to Tony S. the *Queen Elizabeth,* the world's largest ship. "Yeah, that's an American ship," he said proudly. Annoyed by his misapplied pride as much as by his incorrect fact, I told him that this wasn't so. Tony Spaeth said conclusively, "The *Queen Mary*'s American too."

"That's not true!" I shouted.

"Yes it is," he said.

And then, since the cogent argument that should have been suggested by the names themselves didn't occur to me (and might not have convinced TS, anyway), we came to blows.

At only one point in my life to date have I had any confidence in my pugilistic powers, and that was a year after this scrap with Tony Spaeth. Even then, I doubt whether it was as much the balance of height, weight and muscles being right for that brief moment as it was a matter of temperament—of feeling like a fighter; of being psyched into the mood of one who had to win. This was at Fairwood, a camp in Michigan to which TS and I were sent for the summers of 1943 and 1944. I was having a friendly pillow fight with a cabin mate one night after lights out when a counselor walked in. He sent us back to bed with the threat that he would see we had a chance to fight in the camp boxing championships.

He kept his word. I found myself in the midget division eliminations, for which I would certainly never have volunteered, representing the Iroquois. From there it was the intertribe semifinals, and then the big match, where I faced the champion (ten years old, like me) of the Mohawks. The bout took place in the Long House, the large replica log cabin that was used also for Sunday-morning services and Saturday-night dances held jointly with the girls' camp five miles up the lake. A canvas tarpaulin was stretched on the floor to be the ring, without ropes. The fight was to be three rounds of two minutes each; the referee was the swimming instructor. Perhaps my Mohawk opponent, a small carrot-haired boy, with short, firm limbs, was as nervous as I, but he didn't show it. Our hands were immersed in gloves which felt like heavy balloons. We bounced these off each other's fists mostly, for the first round, though the odd blow was landed by accident on shoulder or forehead, and meanwhile the spectating mob of campers yelled at us to slaughter each other.

I held my own in the first round. In the second, Carrot-hair clobbered me with several good blows, one of which got me hard in the stomach. In the third, some of my cabin mates decided that yelling for the Iroquois to win wasn't having much effect. One of them, switching to a new exhortation, shouted "Come on, English!" and this cry was taken up by the rest. The word "English" echoed in my fuddled ears. It made a difference. I was no longer just Tony Bailey, by happenstance a contestant in this silly small-boy boxing match, but the representative of the island people, one of the Few, descendant of Harold,

Henry V, Horatio Nelson and Mrs. Miniver . . . Somewhere out of the misty reaches of the past, from Cadbury Hill, Stamford Bridge, Portchester Castle and the White Cliffs, directed through no very conscious aim (my eyes were blurred and smarting), came the powerfully motivated and immensely lucky swing of arm and gloved fist against Carrot-hair's nose—which abruptly bled. The fight was stopped. English was the winner.

‖ 19 ‖

BEFORE FAIRWOOD, IN THE SUMMER OF 1942, TONY SPAETH
and I were sent to a camp in Ohio, ten miles north of
Chillicothe. "Ideal for boys who do not want to go far
away," said the brochure for Willow Branch Camp,
thereby appealing to thrifty parents of possibly homesick
children in Columbus, Cincinnati and Dayton. Willow
Branch was run by Edward T. Cook, Cornell 1910, U.S.
Olympic Team 1908, Director of Physical Education and
Athletics in the Oakwood schools. At Willow Branch, the
brochure went on, "There are three objectives—to take
excellent care of the boys, to give them a happy, joyous
outing, and to teach them many things which will con-
tribute to their ability, pleasure and enjoyment throughout life . . . Individual attention is given to every boy . . .
A special point is made of good food."

The long summer vacation—nearly twice the length of
summer holidays in England—presumably had a practical
agricultural purpose in the past, but in the industrial,
metropolitan present it has made necessary an alternative
occupation so that parents don't go crazy with children
running in and out of the house all summer saying "What
shall I do?" and "I'm bored." Hence "camp," an American
institution. Willow Branch Camp was built on the shore
of a small lake, within sight of the wooded Mount Logan
hills, which rise roughly a thousand feet above the un-
dulating farmland of southern Ohio. Mr. Cook owned a
thousand acres there. A camp farm provided milk and
vegetables. We were kept busy with long horseback rides

in the hills and swimming and canoeing on the lake. We lived in big tents with wooden floors, though we called them cabins, five boys in each plus a counselor, who was generally a college freshman or high school senior. The entire camp population was thirty-five—an extended family for the Cooks, whose big white frame summer house formed the central lodge.

In Cabin II, my cabin mates were Billy Long, Fritz Nelson, Timmy Espy and Irv Harlemart; our counselor was Gates Thruston, an Oakwood High School football star. Billy Long was also from Oakwood, a friend and contemporary of mine in third grade at Harman Avenue School. Another good but new friend was Joe McKell, whose family helped the Cooks run the camp, and who had a pet raccoon named Alice. Alice lived in a cage at the edge of the woods and her birthday, on June 29, was celebrated like that of any camper whose birthday occurred during the summer, with ice cream and angel food cake all around—Alice ate her share. On Sunday evenings the camp routine called for "bag suppers": paper bags containing peanut-butter and jam-filled rolls, graham crackers and fruit, which we ate at outside tables, and considered a treat. After this a giant watermelon would be handed out for each cabin, carved into moon-shaped slices by the counselor and distributed on the end of his leather-sheathed camping knife.

At Willow Branch we played a great deal of capture the flag—a variant of one of those games of chase and captivity that we played on Talbott Hill. Here we played it in the woods north of the camp infirmary—a cabin with four beds for cases of measles, mumps and acute poison ivy, a native complaint to which I was, for the time being, immune, perhaps partly because of a European ("we are different") disbelief in the fact that one could get an illness from a plant; it didn't last. A dirt road ran into the woods behind this sick bay. We used this for the dividing line between the territories of the two teams, identified one from the other by one team wearing handkerchiefs tied around their arms. Each team had its guards, scouts and runners. The object was to capture the enemy's flag—generally an old shirt tied to a stick—and get it back to base in the heart of one's territory. Any player tagged in enemy territory had to become a prisoner in the enemy base, or ring, and remain there until released by a member of his own side reaching the ring untagged, and freeing him. Once you got into the enemy ring you were at liberty and could not be tagged until you touched the flag. In the ring, you had the choice of freeing a prisoner, if one was there, or going for the flag.

When I was playing capture the flag I wanted my side to win more than I wanted the United States and Britain to win the war. The game began with each team in its own ring, a glade in the woods, forbidden to move until we heard a blank starting-pistol shot echo through the trees. Then for several exciting hours there were long periods of quiet, broken only by the sounds of the woods, birds calling, the occasional snap of branch or twigs, rustle of leaves, and sudden bursts of shouting: "Here comes one! Catch him!" It was tense work being a guard, watching the undergrowth for signs of movement, and being ready for an enemy to dash for the flag. It was neat, being a scout on the lookout for enemy runners, finding a comfortable hideout from which to keep watch, or patrolling a section of woods. It was of course best of all to be chosen as a runner, when one would spend a lot of time crawling and stalking into enemy territory, and then make a sudden final run, with heart pounding, breath loud, into their ring. Being a prisoner—especially if you were captured early on in the game—was boring, though you always had the hope that a runner might get through and free you instead of taking the flag. Once in a while the flag was captured and you continued to sit out in the woods, not knowing the game was over.

The following summer Tony Spaeth and I were considered ready for a bigger and more distant camp—Fairwood, near the town of Bellaire, Michigan. We took the train from Dayton to Toledo, and then to Detroit, where we wandered around the station for an hour while waiting to board the Père Marquette train that was to carry us north, overnight, up the Michigan peninsula. There was something dusty and pioneering about the Père Marquette. The railroad cars seemed to have more wood in them than steel. The seats were covered in heavy, faded plush upholstery. The windows opened, at least in principle. And the name of the railroad brought to mind explorers, missionaries and trappers. On my first trip to Fairwood I was disappointed, waking in my berth on hearing someone shout out "Grand Rapids," and lifting the window blind, to see, beyond my own dim reflection in the glass, merely a floodlit marshaling yard. Where was the booming waterfall, the white water, the log jams? However, when we reached Fairwood early the next day and I saw the thick northern woods and the long lake— Torch Lake—on which the camp stood, I had already forgotten this failure of a name to live up to the dreams it evoked.

Fairwood, three times the size of Willow Branch, had authentic-looking log cabins, housing ninety boys. It taught them to swim, sail, pitch camp, paddle, row, carpenter, and shoot both a rifle and a bow and arrow. There were indoor and outdoor athletics. For achievement we were awarded "letters"—cloth *F*s, to be sewn onto shirts. But the camp specialized in "Wildwood Wisdom"— the name of a book admired by the camp director. Long before *The Whole Earth Catalog* and the ecological move-

ment, we were instructed in making use of nature's natural products. *Wildwood Wisdom* told how one made a
deerskin poncho or a rabbit-fur face mask. We learned
how to make sleeping shelters of branches, notched together, and tripods of green sticks to hold aloft our mess
tins of Boston-style pork and beans. We were supposed to
know how to get a fire started underneath them by winding a string around a pointed stick and then, twisting it
clockwise and then counterclockwise, getting it to spin fast
in a small pile of birch-bark kindling. This produced more
often than not small puffs of gray smoke and no flame.
(Lessons learned: 1. always carry matches with you, pref-
erably in a waterproof container; 2. pork and beans are
all right cold.) We were given tips on the differences
between edible and nonedible plants and berries. In handicraft lessons we made rings out of silver wire and ash-
trays from pewter; one such object, hammered into a
slightly irregular shape by me at Fairwood, still decorates
the top of my mother's writing desk, a useful repository
—since neither of my parents have ever smoked—for paper clips and for postage stamps that have lost their sticki-
ness. Possibly because the object made provokes memory,
I remember making things in a way that I don't remember
talking or feeling.

One other item on the Fairwood curriculum was Indian
dancing. We had lessons on the subject every Monday,
Wednesday and Friday morning at nine-fifteen. And every
Saturday night we gathered in a high-banked arena of
wooden seats for the Grand Council. The Council fire in
the center of the patch of earth was a cunning wildwood
construction, a square of logs with their ends overlapping
—but often doused liberally with kerosene before it was
lit. My thrice-a-week instruction in Indian dance and previous tutelage with Miss Seitner did not qualify me, or
my age group, for taking part in the performance, so I

sat with my cabin mates and watched the older boys dancing around the flames. Drums beat. The dancers wore
feathered headdresses and masks. Heel, toe, heel, toe—
knees raised in a sort of skipping motion; torso and head
alternately bowing forward, leaning back—the forward
progress of each dancer less than the energy being ex-
pended would lead one to expect. The darkness was
warm. The firelight, moving shadows and strange power
of the masks transformed, or nearly so, the senior campers and counselors into what they were pretending to be,
what perhaps for the moment they wanted to be. This was
about twenty years before people generally began to think
of the Indians as exemplars of a more sensitive way of
approaching nature. For most Americans, Indians were
still exotic or savage. But at Fairwood, by means of wood-
craft and dance, the descendants of the dispossessors acquired an unconscious sympathy for those who had been
dispossessed.

Letter from camp:

Sunday

Dear Mother,

We have lots of nice boys in our cabin. Their names are
Jerry Jung, David Hamilton, David Cooper, Bill Whittemore, Allen Whittemore, and myself. We had a dance with
the girls camp last night and I had lots of fun.

We had punch to drink and the naval gunner who sang
on the radio once, sang during the intermission.

We went on an overnight trip the other day and I got
poison ivy on my face. We hiked 23½ miles. I hope you are
well. I am.

Your loving son,
Tony
p.s.   kisses are for you all.

x   x   x   x   x   x   x   x   x   x   x   x   x   x

As Mr. Cook's brochure for Willow Branch suggested, certain things were planted at camp that later thrived. "We hiked 23½ miles." And perhaps because I enjoy walking now, I can see certain moments of that hike as if it were the first walk I'd made—as in some ways it was. Small glimpses of Michigan landscape appear: a strip of roadside, the gravel lying thin on the edge of the newly paved road, and the smell of the fresh tar mixing with the smells of the pine forest, out of which we had just emerged into the hot afternoon sun; a gray barn; an old black car parked alongside it; telephone poles; then into the woods again, mess tins and water bottles jouncing from our belts, and at last the sight of Torch Lake, our lake, shimmering. Not far to go now! *"Thalassa!"* cried Xenophon's men, finally seeing the sea, and we too felt the joy of return, the round trip accomplished.

Torch Lake was roughly fifteen miles long and, across from Fairwood, some one and a half miles wide. The camp owned a collection of boats: a motorboat and several sailing boats that were kept moored off the beach, while on racks, on the shore, were a dozen canoes of various sizes, from simple two-man craft to one "war canoe," which carried eight paddlers. In handicraft classes that first summer at Fairwood we were encouraged to make our own boats. It was a project that excited me. The boats were "flatties"—shallow boxes, with pine sides, backs and fronts, and a Masonite or hardboard bottom. Each side had a fair amount of rocker, so that the bottom, although flat across the beam of the boat, had some curve or shape fore-and-aft. The dimensions were four feet overall length, two feet beam. We laid white lead in the seams and nailed the pieces together. We slapped on white paint. We made simple double-bladed paddles with closet poles and pieces of hardboard. Then we named them. Mine was called *Thunderbolt*. Launching this vessel and stepping into it, I experienced an almost delirious sense of creation and possession, which was not diminished by a small spot of water that appeared beside one seam along the bottom, quickly followed by another spot and then another—my first leak. We had a water carnival and raced our flatties. The crafts instructor said that we could take them home with us when camp ended, but there must have been shipping difficulties or a contrary decision at higher levels, because the flatties stayed at Fairwood, "laid up for the winter" like yachts, when we left.

The second summer we were introduced to sailing. I had, I later realized, a necessity for water and dabbling in it, a need which had been encouraged no doubt from the start by floating bathtub toys—a yellow Bakelite duck, particularly, which sometimes capsized and stayed wrong side up until I made a tidal wave travel down the bath to bring it upright again. There were also the pleasures of sailing my model yacht at Portsmouth on Southsea Pond—the delight of getting the sails and tiller properly adjusted so that the yacht sped on a single straight track across the pond while I ran around to retrieve it; and the apprehensions when the wind suddenly shifted, or a collision occurred with another yacht, which threw everything awry, and then the yacht sat out in the middle of the pond, drifting this way and that—would I ever get it back? From there it was a swift progress to the rowing boats rented out by Mr. Hooper on the beach at Sandown, Isle of Wight, where we went in the summer, and the leisurely

The next letter *adress of camp*
from mome will be Camp Fairwood
from fairwood Bellaire, Mich.
U.S.A.
630 Runnymede
UNITED STATES ARMY
AIR FORCES Dayton, Ohio
June 26, 1944
Dear Mother and Daddy, Sun.

Tomorrow we leave for camp.
and Tony Spaeth and I are
very excited. Our trunks
left on Wednesday with
lots of other boys and girls
trunks who are going to
our camp and nearby camps
. This year I think I
will be in cabin 4 or five
which is the junior cabin.
all cabins below cabin 4
such as one, two and three
are the midget cabins. I was
in cabin three last year.

X From cabin 8 to 13 are the X
X intermedets, and from 13 X
to 17 the seniors. This year the X
sailing instructor is going X
to be a navy gunner X
who is on (specil) special X
leave. X

I got a nifty scout X
ax the other day and X
it is so sharp it chips X
wood so fast I could X
hardly believe my eyes

This after-noon we X
are going out to the Polo X
Club swimming pool. X
It is coldest pool in Dayton X
because it is filled with X
X spring Water. I hope you
X are all well. loving son X
X X X X X X X X X X X Your Tony X X X

aspects of floating a few yards away from the sand while the current slowly bore me toward the spindly iron legs of the pier, and my father eventually dragged me back again abreast of where he and my mother were sitting. And next the fishing skiff at Chatham. But sailing itself, with its new tackle, new terms, was clearly a skill and art of a higher plane. I was going to master it.

Thus in the capable hands of slightly older initiates I was introduced to halyards, sheets and warps; windward and leeward, port and starboard; tacking and gybing. We rowed out from the dock, three or four of us with the sailing instructor. We were at once put to work bailing out the boat to be sailed. The water in the bilges was either the result of rain, dew or a slight leak, and was apparently nothing to worry about if it was slight enough, when it was said to keep the boat sweet. After bailing, we bent on the sails—slipped the slides onto the track that held the cotton canvas to mast and boom, then saw that the rudder was free to swing and that the mainsheet, which controlled the boom, was uncleated so that it would run out when the sail was hoisted. Then we hauled away on the halyards. The sails went up and flapped impatiently in the breeze; the boat fidgeted. It was necessary to look around to see that all was clear—no other boats in the way —before making the jib fill, which pulled the bows around to one side, and letting the mooring line go. The boat heeled, slid forward, moved faster, *sailed*.

Learning and liking were interlocked. I learned how to tie a bowline, among other knots, and haven't forgotten the mnemonic account of the rabbit coming up through the hole, around the tree and back down the hole again. I liked the "blocks"—the wooden pulleys through which the lines controlling the sails passed back and forth several times, doubling or tripling the force one could exert on them. I recognized the reason for dropping—that is, lowering—the centerboard when going to windward, to prevent the boat from sliding sideways under the pressure of the wind, and I soon learned why one ducked one's head, at the shout of "Hard a' lee," as the boom flew over. I liked the gleam of varnish on the spruce spars and mahogany trim of the cockpit, and I took pleasure in the feel of the cotton sails as we furled and unfurled them. I enjoyed the sounds of water made against the bottom of the moving hull, trickling, pattering, slithering past. I liked the way the boats, when alone, with no one in them, swung on their moorings, for the most part head to wind.

We sailed across the lake and then reached down the far shore; tacked into the mouth of a little creek, where we ran aground, hauled up the centerboard, tilted the boat, and sailed off again. Perhaps if one suspected when one embarked that this would be a trial run for many future voyages, then the proceedings would be more portentous: this is an activity that one is about to become addicted to, and there is still time to back out and not get involved. Sailing like few other sports provides an alternative life, with its own anxieties and delights that wipe out the equivalent pleasures and responsibilities of the shore. On the water one would forget one's family, mortgage and career. On Torch Lake there were no complications arising from the fact that one was American, English or German; one was merely a creature of the planet learning how to manipulate the elements of air and water, feeling the happiness that comes from striving for and occasionally reaching a harmony with some of the basic properties of life.

Possibly all this is something I would have acquired later, on Portchester harbor, where my parents lived again after the war, and where I sailed in a small clinker-planked dinghy called a Portchester Duck. But I feel the gratitude to Torch Lake and Fairwood that one feels for first things, for the first kiss or the first book that gives one a dizzy sense of the possibilities of words, the way *Moby Dick* did for me that afternoon I took a Mademoiselle-enforced nap on the upstairs landing and Melville's pages fanned out an array of images and impressions, barely comprehended by me but overwhelming for all that.

I remember a Torch Lake afternoon sail that ended late. We were becalmed for a while. We got tired of paddling. For some reason the camp motorboat didn't come looking for us to tow us in. As the sun went down we heard the camp bugle playing taps for the lowering of the flag. The shore got darker, a black frame around the silver surface of the lake, and the pink in the sky faded. Then the barest breeze shaped the sails and the boat ghosted along toward the lights of the camp, while the sky above slowly filled with stars. Wonder of the sort that hooks one ever after.

‖ 21 ‖

OTTO DRESSED EXPENSIVELY. MANY OF HIS SUITS, SHIRTS AND ties came from Sulka (New York, London, Paris, Palm Beach). Jackets were silk-lined, and his towels and handkerchiefs had the monogram *OLS*. For waiters, doormen, bartenders, taxi drivers, caddies and porters, tips appeared magically in his hand. "Thank you, Mr. Spaeth." "This way, Mr. Spaeth." He enjoyed making money but he also enjoyed disposing of it, though he didn't believe the government should get more than its due, and he had a long-running fight with the Internal Revenue Service about how much that was. In 1953, when I was in New York on a Spaeth-sponsored trip during a university summer vacation, I sat in Otto's office suite in the Sulgrave Hotel, where a connecting door had been created for him through the wall to the Spaeth apartment in the building next door, at 640 Park Avenue, and chatted with him while he bounced a new grandchild on his knee, played rummy with the child's mother, his daughter Marna, discussed my plans to work for the summer in Wisconsin, went over a speech he was to make that evening to the American Federation of Arts, and talked on the phone to the officials of several organizations he was currently helping, one being Walter White of the National Association for the Advancement of Colored People. Otto wrote out a check for $1,000 for them at the end of the conversation.

When credit cards were introduced, Otto had one of the first: the bill in restaurants would come back to him and he would add on a tip and sign his name without interruption to whatever he was saying. "Thank *you*, Mr. Spaeth," said the waiter, handing the card back to him. Otto was known by name in several good New York restaurants, like Pierre's, as well as several German-American eating places where he got many of his favorite dishes to eat. That 1953 summer, when I worked in Wisconsin (weekends at Metamold, trying to sell pictures; weekdays assembling garden furniture and picking apples), Otto's assistant Frank Getlein and I had the occasional use of the company's Chevrolet station wagon and the company credit card, and once every couple of weeks we drove to a big restaurant in the suburbs of Milwaukee called Wolf's Island for a German dinner in Otto's style, at Otto's expense, and indeed in Otto's honor—we often talked while eating T-bone steaks or sauerbraten about Otto's schemes and achievements (Otto at the time being in New York or East Hampton). Frank not long ago told me that Otto once confided to him that he thought he had wasted his life. He had made a lot of money early on; after that, much of what he did was just a game. He thought he should have gone into politics.

However, in a way he did. He was a founder member of Americans for Democratic Action, a pressure group for the enactment of liberal legislation and for the prevention of reactionary excesses. Art politics and religious politics absorbed him. In Dayton, museum directors were constantly coming to see Eloise and him. Influential churchmen paid similar calls. "Monsignor Nabuco is coming to dinner," we would be told, in the same way that, later, we would hear the names of such guests as Father Ford, Catholic chaplain at Columbia University, or young Father Ivan Illich, then priest in charge of a largely Puerto Rican parish in East Harlem. In 1948, when the Legion of Decency was bullying movie producers into nervous self-censorship, Otto attacked them in an article for *Arts* magazine. Cardinal Spellman—from the pulpit of St. Patrick's Cathedral—had just denounced as blasphemous Roberto Rossellini's film *The Miracle,* about a peasant girl who becomes pregnant and imagines that her child will be a new Christ, encouraging the Knights of Columbus to picket the movie theater where it was playing, and Otto's article, written several months before, looked like a defiant reaction to the Cardinal's remarks, which worried Otto, though he knew he was right. The conflict between pickets and long lines of moviegoers at times became physical, and the city closed the show. In the subsequent court case, brought against the city by Joseph Burstyn, the movie distributor, Otto's article was cited in testimony by Burstyn's lawyers as representative of the opinion of outraged intelligent Catholic laymen.

The case went all the way to the Supreme Court, which found for Rossellini, Burstyn and Otto. "Otto was a scrapper," said Frank.

It was through the *Miracle* affair that Frank went to work for Otto. At the time Frank was teaching English at a small Jesuit college in Fairfield, Connecticut, and writing movie reviews for the weekly *National Catholic Messenger,* which Otto subscribed to. Frank wrote a piece praising *The Miracle.* Otto wrote to Frank saying "Drop by sometime." Frank wrote back and said "How about next week?"—the Jesuits, also *Messenger* readers, had just fired him. Otto thereupon hired Frank to help him run the Liturgical Arts Society (of which Otto was then president), the Spaeth Foundation for Religious Art, and various programs Otto had then for promoting business involvement in the arts. For several years Frank served as Otto's cultural henchman and had an interesting if demanding time—Otto frequently called him up at home late at night with ideas for speeches he had suddenly decided to make.

Otto's energy was combined with luck, Frank and I agreed. But luck, we should perhaps have admitted, is in some ways a by-product of energy; if you bustle around, you put yourself in more situations where fortune may favor you. Calling on Iowa farmers out of Davenport, he sold tractors. Traveling out of St. Louis, he found a new market for malt extract. And taking the Spaeth poodle Alex for a morning walk on Park Avenue, when they were living in New York, Otto encountered a beautiful woman also walking a poodle. They met at the same lamppost. The woman was Grace Kelly, then a young film star. (No one else met Grace Kelly while taking Alex for walks.)

Otto also liked making bets, and he liked making people realize that their firmly held assumptions were wrong. Most Americans think they have a comprehensive knowledge of their own country. Otto had a jigsaw puzzle of the United States made of red plastic, the pieces cut out along the borders of each state, but the states having no other identification to indicate which was which. Otto would ask visitors in Oakwood how long they thought it would take them to fit the puzzle together. Most would say confidently, "Oh, five minutes at the outside." Otto, delighted by this answer, would reply, "I bet you fifty dollars you can't do it in ten minutes." He made money on it. Of the very few who managed to complete the puzzle under the time limit, the first was Jerry Adams, son of Philip Adams, then director of the Cincinnati art museum. After that, Otto lengthened the odds, and set the stakes at $5 for five minutes for Midwestern high school students (Jerry was one), who Otto reckoned had a better-than-average knowledge of the outlines of the states.

Of course, when the puzzle was completed there was

little suggestion of those borders in the solid red mass of
the United States. It was this puzzle, which Tony Spaeth
and I got quite good at, that suddenly came to mind
when, nine years after I had last seen it, and a day or so
after that meeting in Otto's Sulgrave office, I found myself
in a four-seater Beechcraft Bonanza with Otto and a
pilot, flying to his factory in Wisconsin across mountains,
fields, forests, lakes and towns, at a less remote height
than an airliner would have taken, and with one state
rolling into another the way they had in Otto's puzzle
when one finally got it put together.

Otto subscribed to—among other publications—*Fortune,
America* (Jesuit-edited) and *U.S. Photo.* The latter often
featured, in those pre-*Playboy* days, artistic photographs
of nude women, posed interestingly but not very informa-
tively in strong effects, say, of sun and shadow. Otto smoked
Kools, a mentholated cigarette. Once a year he would
have a stag session with two or three men friends—a short
vacation in which they would simply move into one or another of their homes (generally 630 Runnymede) for two
or three days and play golf by day and cards by night,
and get through an iceboxful of Pabst. Although, according to his friend Jack Taylor, Otto fitted into the top
rank of Dayton industrialists like a rattlesnake, and some
of them considered him to be a traitor to his group, he
was accepted in various onerous and honorary posts: as
a member of the finance committee and trustee of the
Dayton Philharmonic Orchestra Association, and as head
of the committee at Moraine Country Club which arranged a tournament one year for the Professional Golf
Association, and earned him some kudos from those who
generally thought of him as a dangerous Democrat. For
me, apart from Christmas, the most important day of the
year was one I shared with Otto—January 6, the day between my birthday on the fifth and his on the seventh,

when we celebrated with a cake decorated with the initials *OLS* and *TB*. The number of candles was worked out by methods that varied from year to year, on one occasion being computed from my age divided into his and doubled. We blew out the candles together.

|| 22 ||

In dayton, as in other places to which english children were sent during the war, America had its effect.
Many evacuees did not want to go home. English girls
with English-rose complexions and names like Valerie and
Heather gradually became bobby-soxers, so called after
the thick white cotton ankle socks they wore, often inside
brown-and-white saddle shoes. Their feet beat time to
songs crooned by Nelson Eddy, Frank Sinatra and the
Mills Brothers—songs from America's heartland with lyrics
like"I'm goin' to buy me a paper doll," and "Mairzy doats
and dozy doats and liddle lamzy divey." Hollywood and
Tin Pan Alley; Detroit and the World Series; making the
team and cheerleading; dating; eating ice cream sodas at
a drugstore soda fountain; smoking . . .

Debbie showed Tony S. and me how to smoke one day
in the butler's pantry. It was James's day off. Alongside
the sink was a drawer in which were kept cartons of cigarettes—Kools, Chesterfields and Lucky Strikes. We took a
dark-green pack of Luckies, whose snappy name was backed
up by the insidious slogan "L.S.M.F.T."—Lucky Strike
Means Fine Tobacco—which some advertising genius had
sent forth to work itself into the brain cells of the nation.
Debbie showed us how to hold the cigarette in a poised
manner between two fingers, and how—having breathed
in a mouthful of smoke—to get it to ooze smoothly out
through the nostrils. I felt slightly dizzy at this dusky fore-
taste of countless Old Golds, Gold Flakes and Gauloises
that I was to consume between the ages of eighteen, when

I started smoking regularly, and thirty-two, when I stopped.

Debbie had her own radio. She seemed to me at one point, perhaps when she was twelve and a half and all of two years older than me, to be very grown-up, even with her lovely long brown hair in braids tied at the end with hair ribbons. She had a way of putting a finger against one side of her mouth and pouting slightly, her mouth twisting to one side and her cheeks hollowing into dimples—which made her look thoughtful. I thought it was a pity she was away much of the time at school in Arizona.

And yet comparable to this admiration was the envy I felt for a boy at Fairwood called Winterbotham—English, needless to say, his accent unmodified (at least to my ears) by his stay in America. He was seven years older than me, and he was going back in the autumn of 1943 via Canada to join up and help finish off the Jerries. I didn't know when I would be going back. But perhaps I envied him less for his returning to fight than because he seemed to be all of a piece—English Winterbotham, probably soon to be Flight Officer Winterbotham, as English as Cheddar cheese, Bovril and Hovis. I was already not of a piece. I was two things at least—"English" on occasion, as in that boxing match, and also a regular Oakwood kid. I was double like my doubled name, Tonybailey, needed to distinguish me from Tonyspaeth. I had two sets of parents, with sisters in Dayton and a sister in England. I had a past that was hardly known to my American family and a rapidly accumulating experience here in Ohio that would never be totally conveyable to my parents in England. Otto, for example, had no idea of what it was like to ride a Southdown green double-decker bus to Fareham in the morning and walk up High Street to St. Benedict's School. Similarly, my father would have no conception of how it felt to sit on the fold-down seat in the back of the Cadillac or to be forced to eat asparagus, though he might, given the basic male interest in sports and cars, have been able to put himself in my shoes and understand what it was like to root for the St. Louis Cardinals (as I did) or drool over designs for cars like the postwar Studebakers.

Of course there were many things my mother and father were learning about that I would never find out, or at best have only a glimmer of. For a start, what it was like to send a son, one of two children, three thousand miles or so into the somewhat unknown and certainly the unforeseen. My mother later would say with a wistful smile, "When you've got children of your own you may understand." But I'm not sure that I ever really grasped what it was like for her, and to do so now I would have to magnify the scarcely earthshaking effects of sending one of my teen-age daughters away for a week, and forfeit the familiarity with the transatlantic distance that for my mother must have been so daunting. She had, moreover, no foreknowledge of how the war would turn out. Hitler might successfully invade Britain. I might be stuck in a diminished democratic enclave of a world dominated by the Third Reich. It must have seemed quite possible, as she stood on the steps of Edenholme waving goodbye to me, that she would never see me again.

I didn't worry much about the dangers of war to my parents and Bridget. I assumed that they would be fine, be well, be fit, in accordance with the dutiful expressions of hope to that effect which ended my weekly letters. I could draw pictures of air raids and dogfights over England, even visualize the gunfire and bomb blasts, and not associate them with anyone of my family. Yet the bombs were hitting Southampton, five miles from Park Gate— were exploding and burning not only in the dockyards but in residential streets like Rose Road, where my mother's family lived at number 5. One night the house next door was directly hit. Although windows were smashed and walls cracked at number 5, the Molonys were safe under their Morrison steel table, protecting them from large pieces of ceiling plaster; but the next day my grandfather came out from the city on the train to visit my mother, and as he walked up the unpaved lane from the station, uphill past the fighter-plane repair works, his legs began to disobey his brain. When he reached the gate of Edenholme he could only shuffle and he was unable to speak clearly. My mother put him to bed. We had no phone; she had to cycle a mile to the doctor's. Granddad had had a stroke. My grandmother was summoned by telegram and came out from Southampton; together with my mother she nursed Granddad for the five remaining days of his life.

My father fretted because he was too old for immediate call-up. The bank he worked for wouldn't let him volunteer, and so he had to wait for the war to go on long enough for his age group to be conscripted. Meanwhile he served in the Park Gate unit of the Home Guard—the middle-aged volunteer force whose formation Churchill had proposed in October 1939. It was established in May 1940 under the name Local Defence Volunteers, but soon reverted to Home Guard, Churchill's original suggestion; by the end of June nearly one and a half million men had joined them. In Park Gate, as all over Britain, the local men of property, old soldiers, farm workers, poachers, mechanics and professional men turned out to train, go on route marches and practice with whatever arms they could lay their hands on. In some places it was shotguns and walking sticks, revolvers and brass knuckles. In Park Gate, by some quirk, the local Home Guard unit received an early shipment of Sten guns, a simple short-barreled automatic weapon which looked as if a plumber had made it but which, my father felt, could have done a lot of damage to any invaders. The Home Guard was prepared to block roads and lay hazards across fields and golf courses to deter enemy forces arriving by parachute and glider. Cricket pitches, sacred turf, were dug up and obstructed. Signposts and street names were removed; church bells ceased to ring, for they were to be sounded as warning of invasion. Members of the Home Guard kept watch on the sky and the sea, and they checked vehicles at roadblocks. My father's unit was enlivened by the presence of a local strawberry grower named Billy Cleves who liked to see that he and his colleagues were comfortable on duty. On one occasion he brought along a Primus stove for boiling the tea kettle, and was miffed when ordered to remove the blazing object from the packing case on which it stood—the case being full of hand grenades.

The Home Guard was fortunately never put to the test; its members retained their confidence that they would have come well out of the real thing. The Luftwaffe didn't win air control over the Channel, and Hitler diverted his interest to the East. My father, at last called up, did his basic training in the army, climbed Snowdon in midwinter as part of a workout for becoming an officer, and was commissioned in the Pioneer Corps, which performed all sorts of dogsbody duties. He reached the rank of captain, took part in the bloodless invasion of the Channel Islands, and helped run a prisoner-of-war camp. He had the usual amount of military hurry-up-and-wait, and a good deal of time in which to worry about his wife and daughter at home, and to wonder about me, overseas.

But for my mother, worry was worse. Those events that occurred in the backwater of Park Gate tended to be of the worrying kind: my grandfather's collapse and death; my sister getting whooping cough and then appendicitis and only just reaching the hospital in time; several years of nights intermittently spent with Bridget in the air-raid shelter; and letters, from or to me, getting lost or delayed.

What had happened to the parcel of clothes Eloise had mentioned that she had sent three months before? What could she do for distressed Mrs. Deal, whose son Rupert had been declared missing in action? My mother had the power to imagine how other people felt, and this in most cases meant she spent a lot of time worrying for them. Those quick (for me) wartime years were for her a lifetime of anxieties about all the lives that even so slightly impinged on hers. Her worries included past events that had been successfully resolved or by-passed as far as we were concerned—like my voyage out to America and the London Blitz. Her memory re-created my journey, and her worries then, and although she tried to close it off with such remarks as "Wasn't Tony lucky?," it came back again and again.

My mother stood in queues at grocery shops. She kept a ledger showing cans of food being stored: vegetables, jam, condensed milk, Golden Syrup, gravy, salt, corned beef and lamb's tongues—and ticked them off in the margin as she used them. In the ledger she also kept her accounts: rent £4 a month; local property rates of £9 12s. a year, plus 24 shillings for water; the Edenholme electricity bill was just over £3 for the quarter ending in June 1942. Every month £3 (roughly $12) was sent to the Spaeths to help feed and clothe me, a token amount to the Spaeths but significant to her. For several months in the summer of 1942 two commandos were billeted in the house, and each paid a weekly rent of £1 5s., which must have helped. The garden at Park Gate produced a fine crop of fruit, and my mother bottled gooseberries, plums and loganberries, and she made jam—70 pounds weight of it in 1942, plus 10 pounds of lemon marmalade, all noted in the ledger. She kept a list of those people she sent Christmas cards to, putting first those who were abroad and to whom cards would have to be mailed early.

She gave Christmas tips to the baker who delivered, the dustmen who collected garbage, the grocer's boy, the milkman, the window cleaner and the postman. It was as if these things had to be recorded to help her impose an order on existence that otherwise might not be there.

Just before D-Day, the roads and lanes in all that part of Hampshire were crammed with military vehicles: in Park Gate, a Canadian armored squadron, whose tank crews were lodged in local houses; two at Edenholme. One May afternoon my mother and Bridget were in the garden when a pair of twin-engine Messerschmitts came in low, and my mother saw the bullets or cannon shells thudding into the ground around her as she threw Bridget down and herself on top of her. The planes' fire hit the first in a line of tanks. Ammunition exploded. The Canadians ran out and got their machines going and drove them to a safe distance as the burning tank blew up, shattering back windows in Duncan Road. Mother kept in touch with one of her Canadians; the other was killed in the Normandy landings.

The worry that sat in the back of her mind was me: Was I growing away from them? When and how would I come home?

|| 23 ||

As THE WAR WENT ON, SOME PARENTS OF CHILDREN SHIPPED abroad became restless. They—or at any rate the optimists among them—had thought that the evacuation was to be merely for a while, until the Germans were given a quick comeuppance and the 1930s, relabeled 1940s, carried on as before. Those who had put down their children's names for public schools saw the age of entry approaching and passing and their progeny's chances disappearing of getting on what still seemed then the indispensable ladder of British education and success. Now they wanted to know what was being done to bring their children home. Questions were asked in Parliament. As a result of this, several hundred children were shipped from North America to neutral Portugal by Portuguese ship, and there stranded in Lisbon, unable to get any farther. In the House of Commons, Mr. Hogg (Conservative) asked if the Secretary of State for Air would provide air transport to Britain for these children, and wasn't much assisted by the answer he got from the minister concerned, Sir Archibald Sinclair: ". . . resources . . . strained . . . urgent requirements of the war . . . operations in the Mediterranean now . . . Christmas mail to the troops . . . weather very bad . . . best will in the world . . . I am afraid there will be a long delay."

My parents, too, were anxious to know how the matter stood, and letters were exchanged with the evacuation committee, which had moved from Grosvenor House, Park Lane, to less ostentatious quarters in Gwydir Chambers in

High Holborn, a drab street of insurance firms and commercial offices. The committee's secretary, Miss Noël Hunnybun, told my parents in August 1943 of the difficulties of the Lisbon route and its expense—the fare being £220 for an adult, with an unspecified reduction for children under twelve, as I was by a year in 1944. The chances of getting a berth on the North Atlantic route, the only other way, were negligible, said Miss Hunnybun, as they were reserved for military and government people, or boys and girls reaching the age when they could join one of the services. However, in February 1944 Miss Hunnybun wrote again to say that although the previous conditions still applied, there was "just a possibility that Anthony might be able to return by what we call a special sailing."

This, she went on to explain, was by naval transport. "A few boys have had this opportunity and I might be able to arrange it . . ." The cost was a nominal £10, which covered passage and food. No binding commitments were made about the voyage. Waivers saying that the British government or the Admiralty would not be held responsible in the event of calamity or injury would have to be signed by my parents. No details could be given beforehand, and the port of arrival would be kept secret—though once the children had landed, "opportunities are given to telegraph or telephone their relatives." In mid-September, after my parents had signed and sent back the waivers and their separate agreements, Miss Hunnybun replied with bad news. "I regret to tell you," she wrote, "that special sailing facilities may not be available." Would my parents therefore like me to sail by ordinary North Atlantic steamer, on which an occasional passage could be had for £35? Yes, they said. But the next letter from Miss Hunnybun, on October 25, was a surprise. She wrote to my father at his army post to tell him that she had just received a cable: I was on my way—by special sailing, she believed.

"This is very exciting news, is it not, and I am sure that you and your wife must be very pleased at the prospect of seeing Anthony again. He may turn up at any time within the next ten days or a fortnight, maybe sooner, but we cannot give you any exact date of arrival." For security reasons the committee was not told of the arrival of ships, so she counted on hearing from my parents when I got home, in order that the New York headquarters of the committee could be notified of the happy return. Another letter came to Edenholme from the committee in New York. This was "to point out again the need for secrecy in connection with the return of children to England. Even after Anthony's safe arrival home, it is requested that the arrangements whereby he travelled not be discussed with anyone not directly connected with them."

In the best wartime fashion, my return to England had a code name, Operation Theodore. Who or why Theodore, I never discovered. I had graduated (an ornate word for so ordinary an event) from Harman Avenue School in June and was just getting used to the long corridors of Oakwood Junior High, carrying my books from class to class and turning up for football practice. And suddenly it was goodbye. I said farewell to my teachers and classmates. I gave Fred Young—who used to trade (i.e., swap) posters with me—my poster collection. Harry Ebeling and I exchanged address cards that we had printed on a toy rotary press, with rubber type, I'd been given the previous Christmas. Bill Bettcher and I wished each other luck in future track-and-field events, now that we would no longer be running against each other. Mr. Zook, the Oakwood principal, wrote a "To Whom It May Concern" note so as to smooth my re-entry into the British school system, saying that in the six weeks of junior high I had averaged 90 out of 100. "Tony has a fine attitude toward his work and we think highly of him." I ceded all rights in the newspaper route to Tony Spaeth, and left him many of the things that I could not take with me: half-finished model planes, books, the little printing press, and what really hurt to leave behind, a weighty microscope that Otto had given me—matt black and stainless steel, beautifully engineered by Bausch & Lomb, with tiny geared wheels that enabled one to make intricate adjustments to angle and focus, and a heavy base that held it rock-solid on a table. Through this wonderful device I looked at leaves and snowflakes, the latter placed on a slide which, at Otto's suggestion, had been first cooled in the icebox before being rushed out to the snow and then in again with its fragile cargo. TS and I also examined less immediately perishable matter like pieces of fingernail and lumps of bubble gum.

When it was time to go, Tony Spaeth and I gave each other manly handshakes and promised to write frequently, and Otto gave me a hug strong enough to be remembered for a lifetime. "We will see you again," he said, and the "we" seemed not just plural, encompassing him and his family, but regal, a command that would have to be obeyed. Then Eloise and I boarded the 5 P.M. train for New York, and it was once again the excitement of a Pullman berth, the never diminished thrill of being pulled by a steam locomotive, and in the morning, as I went to the washroom with its spring-loaded taps, the faintly sooty, gritty feel of things; outside, the river with flocks of barges, and then, at 8 A.M., the great station, vaulted with stars.

We stayed at the Madison Hotel—in the East Fifties between Madison and Fifth avenues—and waited for further orders. It was only a day or so of visits to the Automat and the tops of skyscrapers again before we received word to report to the Barbizon-Plaza Hotel, on Central Park South. This hotel served as a shore base for British navy personnel during the war. There I was told I was part of Operation Theodore. And there Eloise handed me over to a woman who was to put me aboard the "special sailing." As Eloise fondly said goodbye, she asked me if there was anything I particularly needed before I sailed. I gave the offer serious consideration. At last I said, well yes, I would like a watch—perhaps from a practical standpoint, knowing that I would need to know the time on a ship (though not realizing yet that timekeeping would be complicated by the fact that as we sailed east we would lose part of an hour every day), and perhaps also out of straightforward eleven-year-old acquisitiveness. Eloise was dismayed by my answer. Where could she get a watch at that moment? However, fortune smiles on those who speak up on such occasions: my lady escort was wearing a chunky Bulova which she was prepared to relinquish. It was slipped off her wrist and onto mine. (Eloise took her name and address and in return sent her several pairs of almost-impossible-to-get silk stockings.)

The ship that I and nearly a dozen other youths joined in Brooklyn on October 21, 1944, was H.M.S. *Ranee*—high-sided, flat on top, coal-gray in color. It was several moments before I recognized it as a ship and not a shipyard warehouse. The *Ranee* had begun life a year and a half before as the merchant vessel *Niantic*, but before she left her builders at the Seattle-Tacoma shipyard, destiny—in the form of the Lend-Lease authorities—intervened. She was to become an escort carrier and be transferred to the Royal Navy. Part of the ship's interior was converted into hangars, elevators and aircraft-maintenance areas. A flight deck covered the entire hull, and from it rose a small superstructure on one side halfway back along the ship.

This was the "island," the captain's castle and the aircraft-control station, containing the wheelhouse, bridge, chart room and signal platform, and with a trellis-work tower of radar and radio equipment sticking up from it. Just below the walkways along each side of the flight deck, small balconies, or sponsons, jutted out, carrying the *Ranee's* armament of two 4-inch guns and sixteen 40mm cannon, which were Bofors or Oerlikon high-angle guns meant for repelling enemy planes. Smoke from the engines was discharged through vents on each side of the flight deck instead of through funnels. When she was operating as an escort carrier, the *Ranee* carried twenty-four aircraft, but on this voyage she was to be a freighter, carrying planes only as cargo. Thus the hangars, huge garages, were filled and much of the flight deck was covered with planes, seventy in all, their wings folded up, crammed together like poultry trussed for shipment—bound for Europe.

We were signed on board. I was handed my copy of my entry certificate as a "Boy, third class," the certificate marked "Unofficial" but recording my height as five foot three, my chest measurement as twenty-nine inches, hair Fair, eyes Hazel, complexion Fresh, and identifying features as "Scar behind the right ear"—memento of a mastoid draining operation at the age of five. Lieutenant-Commander Wynne Jones, a New Zealander and First Lieutenant of the *Ranee* (that is, the second-in-command, popularly known as Number One, Jimmy the One, or the Jimmy), welcomed us in the officers' wardroom. There we were briefed on shipboard routine. We were then shown around those parts of the ship where we were allowed to be and allotted our cabins, in each of which two of us were bunked. Even at my unimperious height of five foot three, everything in the cabin seemed low and confined. There were no portholes, for the cabin was placed on an interior corridor running across the ship. Lagged pipes and con-

AMERICA, LOST & FOUND

duits were fastened below the cabin ceiling. In the top bunk, my berth, I had to be very careful when sitting up so that the mark of a pipe or steel beam wasn't left on my scalp. A gray steel wardrobe included a hanging locker, drawers, a desk and a small safe, for which no one gave us the combination.

In the corridors that ran within the ship, frequent bulkheads had to be negotiated via doorways that could be sealed with watertight doors. When going through such a doorway you had to lift your feet over the high sill and duck your head at the same time. We were informed about signals we would hear from the loudspeakers in the passageways: bells for getting up, falling in on parade, standing easy, presenting ourselves for meals, and piping down, which meant lights out and bed. Reveille was at 0630. Cocoa and biscuits were served in the wardroom to get us underway. At 0650 we were to fall in alongside the forward elevator for Physical Training, then have a bath and change. 0735 was time for breakfast. At 0830 we were to report to our posts to act as messengers and do any jobs that the officers could dream up for us. At 0900 we were to parade with the ship's company for Daily Divisions and Prayers. 0930 Lecture or Instructions. 1030 Stand Easy. 1040 Carry On—a comprehensive term apparently covering the activity that followed a tea break, meaning more instructions, lectures or chores. 1130 Lunch. 1230 Messengers to their Posts once more, and a routine for the afternoon that was similar to the mornings. At 1600 Afternoon Tea. 1630 Games. 1830 Dinner. 2045 Supper. 2100 Rounds. 2130 Pipe Down. On the routine sheet we were each given it said firmly: "All Boys are to be turned-in in their bunks immediately after this Pipe. Duty C.O. will inspect cabins to see that this is done."

That night, as I was getting "turned-in," my surroundings and my anticipation of all this naval routine gave me the feeling that I was part of the war effort at last. My enthusiasm had not been dampened by the bluff petty officer who showed us how to find our way around the ship, instructed us on proper shipboard behavior, and described the *Ranee*'s behavior in a seaway as "something fierce." "One hand for yourself and one for the ship" was the traditional advice he gave. When "Action stations" were sounded, all Boys were to muster in the wardroom. The *Ranee,* we gathered from our guide, was considered by her crew to be what he called a Woolworth carrier, or banana boat, and he advised us not to dawdle if we heard the sharply clanging bells announcing action or any emergency. "These are real coffin ships," he said cheerfully. "If they're hit by a torpedo, they go down like a stone."

‖ 24 ‖

BUT FOR THE TIME BEING THE RANEE FLOATED—AND ALSO
rocked, pitched and rolled. I woke to the dim lights that
were always on, and hearing the ship rattling and vibrat-
ing, remembered where I was. As I stumbled to join my
fellow passengers at the first item on the schedule, I
hung on to the rails and lifelines rigged along the passageways, and I took the first opportunity to find a port-
hole through which I could look out at the heaving Atlantic swell, gray in the gray dawn light—once again the
sea. The convoy, heading northeastward, seemed more
purposeful than that in which I had crossed in the *Antonia*, four years before. The freighters and tankers were
in great number, and there were more warships with
them. Several frigates and corvettes were within view,
bucking along in company with us, collies among the
sheep, and ready to dash off snapping and barking at any
intruders. The white-flecked sea stretched away into haze,
rain squalls and—as the day cleared—the seemingly infi-
nite horizon formed by the curved rim of the world.

Just what the *Ranee*'s captain had said when informed
that he was to carry eleven boys back to the mother country, I can now imagine. But since we were by nature en-
thusiasts of planes and ships, our delight in being where
we were possibly made our presence less irksome among
men who were trying to get on with running a ship and
winning the war. The *Ranee*'s officers and men seemed at
any rate pleased to show off to us their occupations—
whether it was the radar officer with his electronic equip-

ment or an A.B. with waste cotton and oil cleaning the barrel of a Bofors gun. The prescribed message-carrying was clearly a job invented to keep us busy, and for a while kept the officers busier inventing messages to be carried. The prayers and announcements that started the day reminded me of camp, though the PT that followed took the form of gym on the forward elevator, and then running around the open part of the pine-planked flight deck if the sea was sufficiently calm. Several of the officers told us, under the heading "Lecture," of their experiences in various parts of the world; there were films and slide shows. It might have been sensible if we'd been briefed on life in Britain, to remind us of what we were coming back to: V-1 buzz bombs, or doodlebugs, and V-2 rockets, Hitler's last chance; powdered eggs and books printed on dirty oatmeal paper; austerity; gray flannel shirts that felt scratchy, and socks that needed elastic garters to hold them up at knee height; season tickets; single-element electric fires that warmed you if you stood directly in front of them; scanning Latin verse; new nicknames, in many cases naturally "Yank"—but all in all, a life of such difference that it would seem brand-new and not as hard to adjust to as might have been expected.

The *Ranee*'s radio operator told us about Morse code, and a signaler showed us how to send messages with an Aldis lamp to nearby ships. We watched gunnery practice, and afterward were allowed to sit in the gunners' dished-steel seats, turning the handles and looking through the gun sights, imagining attacking planes coming at us. And it was while sitting in the cockpit of one of the Chance-Vought-Sikorsky Corsairs, lashed down at the aft end of the flight deck, that I suddenly missed Tony Spaeth. It was an eleven-year-old's sense of loss—mostly a matter of feeling "Golly, how TS would envy me if he knew what I was doing!" But I also wished that he were there too; he would have loved it. The big naval fighter plane, designed for carrier use, had gull-shaped wings that folded up overhead so that the planes took up less deck space between flights. I gazed at all the dials and instruments. I sat back in the high-shouldered seat with all its straps and attachments, held the oxygen mask to my face, and looked overhead for Zeroes and Messerschmitts. The aircraft rigger who was showing me the plane pointed out the button for firing the cannon, and the controls that made the plane bank and dive and climb. The joy stick had a little funnel on top, for the pilot to pee into—long-distance missions had strains I hadn't considered.

Because no planes were flying off the *Ranee* on this voyage, several large cabins were not being used. We sat and read in the Operations Room, where one wall was covered with corkboard on which charts could be put up and pins stuck in to show pilots the positions of a convoy, escorts and U-boats. Next door was the Ready Room, with a blackboard marked out in spaces for information to be chalked up about weather, wind, sunset, moonrise, enemy intelligence, and the like. This was the place where pilots, observers and gunners sat playing poker while waiting for the call "Hands to flying stations!," which was the order to scramble. Here, sitting in the aircrew's fixed, red leather chairs, we played game after game of Monopoly while the *Ranee* swayed and rumbled across the ocean. The game had a British board. Since we were sailing east, it made sense that we were getting familiar with London topography rather than continue to rattle around the streets of Atlantic City, as I had done when playing in Oakwood with Dricka Haswell and her brother. Now Mayfair and Park Lane were valuable again, and the London Midland and Scottish Railway's dark-crimson livery came to mind for

Anthony Bailey

the first time in four years as I forked out £200—pounds, not dollars—for King's Cross station, next to Euston station, from which I'd gone north from London to Liverpool.

Although America was disappearing steadily behind us, we celebrated Halloween on October 31 at a party given by the *Ranee*'s officers. They were often informally dressed in old gray flannels, turtleneck sweaters and Wellington boots, but on this occasion cast all seniority aside and entered into the spirit of trickery. As we arrived in the darkened wardroom a weird wailing could be heard, and several ghosts jumped out on us. Our heads were ducked as we attempted to bob for apples. But later, after ice cream and cake, when the officers were having dinner, we took our revenge. The technique of pieing a bed was something most of us had learned in America. Refinements were to put various objects inside the sheet that was folded over halfway down the bed. So when the First Lieutenant and his colleagues had turned back into adults and were drinking pink gin or a glass of beer before dinner, we sneaked into their cabins and worked fast. In the First Lieutenant's bed we squeezed out a tube of toothpaste and then put his toothbrush and hairbrush between the pied sheet too, for his toes to meet.

At the Sunday parade of the ship's company, two days before, I had been admonished. My conduct sheet recorded the fact: "Tony Bailey was guilty of an act to the prejudice of Good Order and Naval Discipline in that he failed to comb his hair and polish his shoes." I was therefore "cautioned." Despite this misdemeanor, my final character assessment on the unofficial and not very serious *Ranee* report was "VG," and my Efficiency was rated as Superior. Under General Remarks, which called for comments on intelligence, initiative, energy and powers of command (or would have done in the case of a proper crew member), Lieutenant-Commander Wynne Jones overlooked the

havoc wreaked in his bunk and wrote "Bright & intelligent. Fond of soap and water, and enjoys doubling round
the flight deck. Can do his share of eating at meal times."

We tumbled into our bunks after the party. Pipe Down
on Allhallows eve was as usual at 2130. Asleep, I had no
spooky dreams, no intimations of life being on a short
thread. The warning, when it came, had to pierce deeply
into my slumbers. The clamor of the alarm bells ringing
action stations was, in fact, just ending as I woke up. I
heard almost the echo of the alarm—reverberations of the
third and final call, as it turned out—and for a second
wondered if it was part of a dream. Then I looked down
into the bunk below—my cabin mate was gone. The door
was open. The ship's engines continued to throb, but perhaps more urgently than usual, like heartbeats speeded up.
I clambered down from my bunk, flung my trousers and
shirt over my pajamas, grabbed my inflatable life jacket
and dashed out into the passageway, turning left into the
fore-and-aft corridor that led to the wardroom. No one
was to be seen. As always, the strong engine-room smell
wafted up from within. I came to the first of three
athwartship bulkheads between me and the wardroom,
and found the watertight door firmly closed, sealed with
six big clamps. It didn't occur to me that it might be conduct prejudicial to the safety of the *Ranee* to tamper
with them. I was scared. "Coffin ship" and "sink like a
stone" were the phrases in my head. I got to work on the
handle of the first clamp, hung on to it with my full
weight, and felt it swing slowly open. The next handle was
higher, harder. The third handle wouldn't budge. I
thought of the U-boats out there, the convoy changing
course, the escorting warships each zigzagging, and torpedoes whirring through the water toward the impossible-
to-miss flank of the *Ranee*. I tugged and tugged. At last the
handle moved, the clamp turned. Then the next. It all

took ages. I had just the strength. How I wished someone would come and help me. All around there was just
the steady rumbling and rattling of the ship that at any
moment might explode into fire and steam and the ultimately quenching inrushing torrents. I was still at work
on the last clamp of the first door when it suddenly
budged, turned from the other side and opened to reveal
a petty officer, sent to find me. The roll call of boys had
been taken in the wardroom and disclosed my absence. He
made fast the door and led me back to the wardroom
through the other two bulkheads, clamping those doors
shut as well behind us.

That was effectively the end of the excitement as far
as I was concerned. Fear vanished in company and ex-
planations I had to make about where I had been. Cocoa
and biscuits came from the galley. There was a feeling of
confidence that we would be led, if necessary, to the deck
where the Carley floats and ship's boats hung along the
walkways. And soon there was "stand down" (the naval
all clear), and word that there had been sonar contact with
a submarine, but the sub hadn't got any of us, and we—our
informant thought—hadn't got it. As we climbed back into
our bunks my cabin mate said to me, "I thought you'd
heard the alarm."

THEN it was autumn and northern waters. Gray seas, gray
clouds. "D'ye ken John Peel who is far, far away?" We
rolled the dice and crossed our fingers that we weren't
going to land on Mayfair with its hotel. Long days, despite the routine and the games, toward the end of the
voyage, and possibly I remembered them a few years later
at fourteen, when I had a spell of being interested in becoming a naval officer, and got the forms for applying
for a place at the Royal Naval College, Dartmouth; but
eventually I decided that long periods at sea weren't for

me—there were other ways of satisfying my thirst for salt air, sea water and boats. The convoy sailed around the north of Ireland and into St. George's Channel, and the *Ranee* now on her own moved slowly up a wide lough to a black-gray city with dark shipyard cranes hovering over the docksides. Belfast. Rain fell. Smoke from coal fires rose from thousands of chimneys. The Corsairs were unloaded. Then with an empty flight deck the *Ranee* ill-advisedly plunged out into St. George's Channel for the short final stage to the Clyde and ran into the worst conditions that area had known in November for many years. We hove to behind the Isle of Arran in the Firth of Clyde and waited thirty-six hours for the gale to abate: a night, a day, another night.

At least I wasn't seasick, as the *Ranee* rolled like the proverbial village drunkard on a Saturday binge. Seasickness also came a few years later, coeval with naval ambitions—and remained as a constant threat on small or big boat voyages when those ambitions had lapsed. Late the next, misty morning the *Ranee* sailed up the Clyde, the river banked with lovat-green hills, to the grimy waterfront of Greenock; shipyards, ships, tugs. The boys of the *Ranee* were signed off after tea; autographs were scrawled over the manila envelopes containing our brief and undistinguished certificates of service. I shook hands with the officers and went down a gangplank to a dockside building where a small wavy-haired woman hugged me—her action convincing me, after a few moments' reflection, that she must be more than the friend of the family or aunt I first took her for. In the crowded overnight train going south to England, I slept against my mother's shoulder.

‖ 25 ‖

I BEGAN TO WRITE THIS ACCOUNT AS AN AID TO MEMORY, hoping to recapture and therefore preserve some of my past before it became irretrievable. Some things, however, have already vanished. I am dimly aware of them, hovering tantalizingly just beyond the antennae of remembrance, waiting for the right prod or nudge from present experience, or for the sudden tilt of mind or unconsidered action that stirs up the dust and reveals a little more of the past. But I am left, too, with several bits and pieces over, that I need to pile up here—tidily, at any rate, at the edge of the puzzle. The U.S. Committee for the Care of European Children finally dissolved in the summer of 1953 (when—thanks to continued Spaeth interest in me—I was in Wisconsin picking apples and selling pictures). The ultimate total of children helped by the committee to the end of 1952 was 4,122, a figure which included refugees, orphans, displaced persons and thirteen "stowaways accepted for care." By the war's end 1,315 children had arrived in the United States through the agency of the committee; that number included 42 Spanish children, 209 German children, and 860 English children. The model railroad in the basement at 630 Runnymede Drive was given to an orphanage in 1948, when the Spaeths sold the Oakwood house and moved to New York City. James and his wife, Sugar, went to work for the Haswells at that time, and stayed with them thereafter.

Coming back was a wrench for many children. Knowing that to be a possibility, some parents went to con-

siderable lengths to make their sons and daughters feel
welcome. Old toys were dug out of attics. Insofar as rations
allowed, what had been a favorite food—bubble and
squeak, toad in the hole, spotted dick—was produced and
often didn't meet with the expected enthusiasm. One father, an owner of land in Sussex, planted a line of maples
to remind his son of the North American fall foliage he was
sure the boy would miss, and no doubt the warmth of the
gesture was remembered despite the failure of the maples
to go quite as red and gold in English soil and weather.
Some parents and children were wary of one another; it
took a while to recover familiar bearings. And some parents did what they had been dying to do: greeted their
children and sent them straight off to boarding school—
perhaps fulfilling what the child felt to be the orthodox
pattern of life but almost (a child might think as he un-
derwent this second rupture) as if it were not good for
parents and their offspring to see too much of one another.
There was sometimes an unbridgeable gulf, particularly
between fathers and teen-age girls—they had, in several
senses, "grown away"; they never managed to cross the
divide again. Eventually many of the evacuated children
returned to live in America and Canada, and make their
lives there. A few felt always that they had gained an un-
fair advantage by avoiding the toughest parts of the war,
though of course it was not in their power to do anything
about it.

MY classmates at Oakwood junior high went on to the
varied pleasures and regrets of American school life—to
football games, college board exams and homecoming
balls. (At the seventh-grade Halloween Fancy Dress
Party, which I missed by two weeks, Jane Rich won first
prize as an opera star. Johnny Houk came second as a student nurse.) Tony Spaeth now lives in Rye, New York,

with his wife and four daughters; he is a vice-president for marketing of a large New York City bank. My friends Harry Ebeling and Fred Young still live in Dayton—Harry in Oakwood, a few blocks from Harman school, and Fred a few miles farther out, in a farmhouse built when that part of Ohio was first being settled in the 1820s. Both Fred and Harry are successful lawyers.

I dallied with the idea of studying law. I was granted a scholarship by an Oxford college which seemed to understand that that was my intention, but which admitted me, I later learned, less on the basis of my exam papers in Latin, history and French than an essay I wrote on the set subject of "A Fête or Festival." What came to my mind as I sat in the college hall staring at the blank writing paper was a fair Tony S. and I had been taken to at the Montgomery County fairgrounds, on South Main Street, celebrating the hundredth anniversary of Dayton as a city—the centennial was a spectacular mixture of circus, rodeo, historical pageant and fairground side shows. Perhaps I put into my essay not just a vivid recollection of the fair but a sense, which the historians among the examining dons may have appreciated, of a time and place not that long before but already, as far as I was concerned, lost. When I went up to Oxford after two years' national service in the army, I read—that is, studied—history, at least in principle, for I spent a good deal of time reading other things that took my fancy and writing poems and prose pieces; and eventually I found that I had decided, or that a decision had been taken in and around me, about what I would do, which was write. Like Tony Spaeth I have four daughters. They were born in America, to which I returned on leaving the university, looking for the continuation of the life that my American childhood might have prepared for me, and where I lived for the next fifteen years; and so I have entangled them too with that country, and entangled them with England as well, where we live most of the time now. I have—I sometimes think—lost America again. And, as before, I feel a need—which perhaps I will always have to try to satisfy—to regain and rediscover it.

There are advantages and disadvantages in this divided loyalty. I think occasionally that although in some respects having two countries in one's life hastens the growing-up process, in other respects it means that one takes twice as long to mature, to learn how to cope with and integrate one's double childhood. I sometimes think that I am two Tonys, too. Certainly the experience has left me with a sense of being different, of being a passenger still on a special sailing, which has outlasted the usual but perishable feeling of uniqueness a child has. From time to time this sense of difference—shared, I gather, with many others who were evacuees—promotes self-consciousness or an awareness of distance from those who are simply one thing or the other, British or American. It means that people are occasionally unsure of me, and of my background; a man in a Hampshire shop the other day, hearing me ask for something, said, "You must be from Canada." It gives one a frequent fit of melancholy or nostalgia—when in Britain missing America, when in America missing Britain. But I set against these drawbacks, if that is what they are, not just a greater variety of choice and experience I have enjoyed but an impetus derived from those four childhood years in Dayton. I got from Otto and Eloise a belief in the perfectability of life, or should I say, alongside original sin and man's animal nature, a belief in the need to seek such an ideal? In cardplaying terms, one should now and then shoot for the moon.

There are also the pleasures in having a family on both sides of the Atlantic. When I got back to Park Gate it became my duty to write to Otto and Eloise, just as I had written to my parents from Dayton. The bond stayed firm.

And now when I visit America I always go to see Eloise, who continues to live in Manhattan, and once in a while in her apartment I find myself being introduced, or rather reintroduced, to people—there for drinks, perhaps—who knew the Spaeths in Dayton. With a gesture toward the forty-seven-year-old man at her side, Eloise will say to her friends, "And I wonder if you remember Tony Bailey, who was the little English boy who stayed with us during the war?"

I find that things continue to come back to me. For example, not long ago while leafing through a magazine, I realized that the patterns in an advertisement made me suddenly see the wallpaper in the front hall at 630 Runnymede—the design of small classical temples among groves of trees, silver on brown-gray; and half closing my eyes, I could see Otto standing there, at the foot of the stairs, not knowing that Tony S. and I were within earshot, hiding under the billiard table, on whose precious green cloth we had just spilled model-airplane cement—and Otto calling up to Eloise, at the head of the stairs, "You'd better tell the boys I looked for them but had to go without them. I wanted to give them a last run in the La Salle."

The front door slams, and the car starts up, and Tony S. and I look at each other ruefully, forever.

AFTERWORD

When this book was first published, nineteen years ago, its author was congratulated on his "near total recall." His memory was wonderful. Well, I now want to confess that it had some help. The acknowledgments should begin with immense thanks to my mother, whose secretarial training—and possibly a sense of the eventual needs of history—led her to save everything on paper pertaining to her son and the events described heretofore: letters and telegrams from the Spaeths, and Roy Bower; letters from me; photographs; correspondence to and from the American Committee for the Evacuation of Children; receipts for passport photographs; camp badges and trophies; Royal Naval certificates (unofficial); school reports . . . That was the foundation. And when, browsing through a cardboard box full of this stuff a few years earlier, I thought there might be a book in it, I also realized that I would need even more material to make something of more than personal interest. I put to work my twenty years of experience at that point as a reporter for *The New Yorker*—William Shawn's *New Yorker*—and did the visits and interviews and research that underlie most worthwhile pieces of seemingly spontaneous "fact" writing. I spent a lot of time in libraries on both sides of the Atlantic, reading official histories, books on the Blitz and on convoys, a biography of Marshall Field III, and documents dealing with evacuation. I visited Dayton for the first time in many years and looked up newspaper accounts of the arrival there of the English children. I called on friends, last encountered more than thirty years before. I walked around Oakwood and followed the route on which I had cycled many afternoons after school, delivering copies of the Dayton *Journal-Herald*. I sat down with my former grade-school classmates and a bit later with Eloise and Tony Spaeth and got them talking about the wartime years, the "duration." Many things people think they have forgotten come back in conversation. I delegated some areas of inquiry: for instance, to Fred Young in Ohio I gave the job of determining the rules of Kick the Can, the outdoor game we used to play. Harry Ebeling was my agent for digging up various happenings at Harman Avenue Grade School. At home in England, the subject of children in wartime was introduced rather frequently by me into social chat, and if anyone responded with "Oh, I was evacuated," questions followed, memories were prompted, and notes jotted down when I got home.

The actual writing had many false starts. On and off since I became a writer, I'd attempted to pen pieces of my "adventure," but never successfully. I needed the critical mass of knowledge that my mother's archive and my research and reporting activities brought me. And I needed to find the right tone, the right attitude to my seven-to-eleven-year-old self and those around me, and the right way of organizing my material, which ended up for the most part being parcelled in thematic bundles. The right moment for plunging in and dog-paddling forward came in the late 1970s. We—my wife and I and four young daughters—had returned to England in 1971 after some years of living in New England, and I was getting over giving up America for the second time. I missed America as I had after returning from the Spaeths in 1944, maybe even more so, or more consciously. But I knew that for reasons to do with family, blood ties, the "old country," and who I ultimately might be (somewhat examined in a sequel to this book, *England, First & Last*), coming back was necessary—even if in 1971 when it was a decision I had some control over, it was a difficult move. There were sacrifices of comfort and opportunities to be made in exchange for proximity to my by-then elderly parents and contact with my native, though overcrowded, turf. At any rate, for several reasons, the time had come in the late 70s when sufficient memories were retrieved and the ink flowed from my Parker more steadily than it had in Dayton from a Christmas-gift Schaefer in weekly letters home.

As publication approached, a few authorial nerves began to jangle. Autobiography can be a self-indulgent exercise. I was slightly worried about the reaction of Eloise Spaeth (Otto was dead), because she'd given the impression, when answering my questions about their life in Dayton, that she thought any focusing on Spaeth wealth and how Otto made his money distasteful, and possibly—she had never much liked living in Dayton—the whole subject was a bit parochial, wasn't it?

It may have helped with Eloise that the *New Yorker* in two consecutive weeks ran long chunks of my opus, and when the book itself appeared soon after, to a generally very generous press, friends and people she hadn't heard from in years called and wrote to say how thrilled they were to read about Otto and her. Some of the most severe comments in those reviews were to the effect that the Tony Bailey story was Chekhovian rather than Tolstoyan in scale—it was too short; it ended too soon. Moreover, did any child deserve such a charmed life amid the horrors of the Second World War?

I, too, received many letters, more than for anything else I had written, from people in America and England (where publication followed), and a few correspondents were a bit snippy about my altogether too-idyllic experience. Where was the trauma? One, evacuated to Pennsylvania, had been taken in by a childless couple, the foster mother turning out to be a head case, and horrors followed. A few couples may have thought that they could exorcise their own problems by giving refuge to an English child. Another letter writer, evacuated from the East End of London to the southern counties of England and no further, quite reasonably wanted to know why I had eluded a similar fate and instead gone to—though he didn't put it this way—an undeserved paradise in the Midwest. Had the notorious British class system, and American falling-in with it so that like-to-like placement rules weren't overstretched, had anything to do with this? I replied that I couldn't deny that class or status or professional standing of parents had been a basis for choosing the children on the scheme that sent me. And an important factor was whether a host family could afford, and had the extra room, to look after an evacuee; if children were, as intended, going to be placed with families of generally similar circumstances, there was less chance of poor British children being sent to the United States. But in any event, the gulf between the way the Spaeths lived and the way the Baileys lived had been deep enough. That particular correspondent wrote from the Eastern seaboard, to which he had emigrated postwar, and had evidently prospered.

Fortunately, the greatest number of letters came from former evacuees, many now living in the United States, who were grateful for *America, Lost & Found*. I had, it seemed, also told their story. I had caused them to remember their lives with American families and they were delighted this memory-jogging had happened. Many wrote to give me details of experiences that were of course a little different from mine, and of other aspects of those years they valued and had recaptured. Kool-Aid and Crackerjack were common but not the only madeleines. One woman reminded me that the linguistic fertilization had been two-way: while I was learning words like "neat" and "snappy" in Dayton, she, aged eight in Bedford, New York, had got her classmates to adopt the word "wizard" as the best and latest thing in terms of praise. Although a surprising number had returned to live in the United States in adult life, many of those who resided in Britain had remained in close touch with their American wartime families. Just about every one of my correspondents remarked on how they had had to deal with divided loyalties, feeling both British and American, missing one place when in the other, and having to cope with everything being double thereafter—two countries, two families—and never again being able to be completely wholehearted. But, overall, weren't we lucky? We were a bit "displaced," but—most agreed—the privileges and benefits arising from our complicated condition outweighed the disadvantages.

In Dayton, where a number of my wartime pals still lived, the reception was also mostly kind. My old friends were happily not offended to find themselves in a brief limelight. (Having a grade-school buddy turn into a writer years later could open who-knows-how-many cans of worms.) Generally the book was welcomed as a celebration of American, or rather Dayton, hospitality. There was one pesky question as to whether I'd got the Pledge of Allegiance correct in its then form. No, *mea culpa*; but now fixed! And what about my references to "Runnymede Drive"? An otherwise laudatory column in the Dayton *Daily News* found fault with the celebrated Bailey memory on that score, noting that the present usage, with a longish history, was Runnymede *Road*. Homer nods? In fact (I did some hurried re-checking), sometime during the war the Oakwood Highway Department seems to have changed the signs, so that brick-paved Runnymede DR became Runnymede RD. Letters written by the Spaeths went from using mostly Drive to mostly Road. Asphalt surfacing at

Anthony Bailey

some point followed. But—forgive the jubilation—I regarded the clinching item in this topographic tussle to be a report in the *Oakwood Press,* found deep in my mother's box, noting the arrival in October 1940 of young Tony Bailey at the home of Mr. and Mrs. Otto Spaeth "at 630 Runnymede Drive."

The toughest question remains for all of us who went: what would we have done, had we been in our parents' shoes in 1940? Although it is hard in peacetime to dwell on the anguish of sending one's child away, and harder perhaps to imagine the worries about an imminent Nazi invasion and occupation, both sets of concern would have been in my mother's mind, fidgeting back and forth, back and forth; and probably it was only her thoughts of American friends, American kindness, from her days at the consulate in Southampton, that tipped the scales. She bravely decided, Tony should be sent. She wrote, in a "Baby Book" in which she had recorded my weight at birth and childhood ailments such as tonsilitis, "Tony sailed to the U.S. on Sept. 15 1940. It was very hard to let him go but for *his* sake we did so." But I think that in many ways my mother never got over that four-year separation. When I came back, that crucial continuity of ordinary, day-by-day events, leading to the present, that parents usually take for granted, was no longer hers—or mine. I saw it, as I've written elsewhere, as a sort of veil or curtain between us, which it took an extra, almost unnatural effort to pull aside. It may have made her a bit fussier in her care for me as an adolescent, and that naturally made me dismissive of her solicitude.

My parents and foster parents are no longer here or there. Otto died first in 1966; the Kools cigarettes he liked so much were blamed. My mother died in 1987 and my father in January 1998. In September of the same year Eloise Spaeth died, aged ninety-six, at her house in East

Hampton, Long Island. I flew over the by-now familiar Atlantic to her funeral. As readers will see, I dedicated this book originally to all those who sent us and took us in, but I'd like to amend that now and dedicate this edition specifically to these four people.

About the Author

ANTHONY BAILEY has written twenty books. They include a sequel to this memoir, entitled *England, First & Last*, and also *In the Village, Rembrandt's House, The Outer Banks, The Thousand Dollar Yacht, Major André, The Coast of Summer,* and, most recently, *Standing in the Sun: A Life of J. M. W. Turner.* He was for many years on the staff of *The New Yorker.* He now lives most of the time in England but travels to North America every year.

1